2001

Meeting the ADD Challenge

A PRACTICAL GUIDE FOR TEACHERS

Steven B. Gordon
Michael J. Asher

Research Press
2612 North Mattis Avenue
Champaign, Illinois 61821

Cover design by Doug Burnett
Composition by Graphic Composition, Inc.
Printed by McNaughton & Gunn

ISBN 0-87822-345-2
Library of Congress Catalog No. 94-65554

Contents

Figures and Tables

FIGURES

TABLES

Acknowledgments

We would like to acknowledge the countless numbers of children, parents, teachers, and school administrators with whom we have had the privilege of working. The case examples used throughout this book are real, although some names and identifying data have been changed to protect these individuals' privacy. We are most grateful for the opportunity to work with so many wonderful people.

Special appreciation is due to Norrine Scherler for carefully typing the many drafts of the manuscript, and to Karen Steiner, our editor at Research Press, for pulling it all together.

I (S. B. G.) would like to thank my children, Jennifer and Michael, for providing me with firsthand knowledge of the joys and sorrows of parenthood. This experience has greatly enhanced my ability as a psychologist. I am also very fortunate to have the love, support, and intellectual partnership of my wife, Rita. Finally, I want to acknowledge my parents, Jack and Kit, who gave me the gift of life and the enthusiasm with which to live it.

I (M. J. A.) would like to thank the educators I have worked with over the years who have helped me attain my present professional level. I thank my children, Peter and Adam, for teaching me so much about parenting and for increasing my empathy for what other parents experience. As well, I thank my parents, Carl and Patricia, for their encouragement over the years. Finally, to my wife, Susan, for her love, faith, and support—my sincerest love and gratitude.

1   Overview: Three Case Examples

EXAMPLE 1: GEORGE

George, age 8, exhibited a number of behavioral and academic difficulties. Ms. A., his third-grade teacher, described him as a student unable to stay in his seat or refrain from bothering other students. Ms. A. felt George commanded an inordinate amount of her time and was disturbed that she was unable to give the other children in class the attention they needed.

Due to the problems George created when unsupervised, Ms. A. could not allow him to go to the bathroom alone or to line up for activities outside the classroom without an adult to monitor him. Predictably, George regularly got into trouble in the lunchroom and on the playground because Ms. A. was not there to watch him.

These symptoms of Attention Deficit Disorder (ADD) are highly noxious not only to teachers but also to other students. Sometimes called "garlic symptoms," these characteristics often interfere with teachers' ability to present lessons and create an environment that will enhance other students' learning. Other students often see such behavior as disrespectful, silly, or "bad."

Many children with ADD have significant problems in unstructured situations and in the absence of an adult.

Ms. A. was concerned that George might have a bladder problem because he would ask to go to the bathroom at least a dozen times before lunch. She had also stopped giving George a pencil at the beginning of each day because his constant sharpening would shrink it to an inch and a half by mid-morning.

These commonly reported behaviors often reflect the child's need for movement.

George also had serious academic problems. One of his biggest problems was in completing assignments. His desk was a mess, and he often stuffed incomplete and sloppy work in the back of it, where it would remain indefinitely. In addition, he called out unsolicited comments and answers to the teacher's questions and rarely followed directions given to the class.

Poor academic work, which may be due to an underlying learning disability, suggests the need for further investigation and often requires a learning evaluation by a specialist.

Excessive calling out may be a behavioral manifestation of impulsivity.

Since the beginning of school, Ms. A. had talked with George on numerous occasions about complying with classroom rules. She had placed George's desk next to her own, at the back of the class, in an attempt to reduce his constant touching of other students.

Ms. A. and George's parents had met several times to discuss intervention options. These conferences resulted in three reward programs that used stickers and tokens as incentives for George to improve his academic performance and comply with classroom rules. Each time they tried a program, there would be a few weeks of initial success followed by George's returning to his old behaviors. Punishments both at home and at school were increasing in severity, and all adults who came in contact with George were becoming frustrated by his erratic behavior and inconsistent interest in the reward programs.

Behavior modification programs often go through an initial "honeymoon period."

Inconsistency is another hallmark of ADD.

At her wit's end, Ms. A. referred George to the school district's psychologist in the hope that an evaluation could take place promptly. She thought that removing George from her class would be beneficial to both him and the rest of her students.

Some teachers assume that children with ADD need to be in a segregated classroom.

George's mother had asked for an evaluation once before but had been refused because George was not working far enough below grade level. Had all the teachers' reports been considered, it would have been discovered that George was having difficulties from the moment he arrived at school to the end of the school day. When Ms. A. requested the evaluation, she underscored the need for haste. Unfortunately, George was placed on a 3-month waiting list for testing.

Children with ADD who are not far behind academically and are not disruptive often fail to get the help they need.

George lived with his mother and father, Mr. and Mrs. W., and two older siblings. His mother, age 34, worked as an accountant, and his father, age 36, was employed as a computer programmer. George's brother and sister, ages 14 and 11 respectively, had always been considered good students by their teachers.

Mr. and Mrs. W. were in disagreement as to the need for a referral. They had been receiving unfavorable comments from George's teachers since he was in preschool, but only Mrs. W. acknowledged openly that George, whom she described as "a handful," was very different from her other two children. Mr. W., on the other hand, thought that George's teachers and mother only needed to be more strict. He asserted that all George required was a "swift kick to get into line." Mr. W. described George as a youngster "with a lot of energy" and, in fact, recalled that he himself had displayed similar characteristics as a child.

It is not uncommon to see disagreement between parents as to the nature of the child's problems and the need for formal evaluation.

The chronic nature of the problem helps one diagnose ADD.

Fathers often complain about the lack of discipline and feel that a stricter approach will solve the problem.

ADD is more common among family members than among those in the general population. It is commonly believed that ADD is passed on from fathers to sons.

Because George had recently been asked to leave two after-school programs, Mrs. W. felt the need to switch from full- to part-time employment to provide more home supervision. She was having considerable difficulty managing George's behavior, which she described as "wild and uncontrollable." Most of their problems occurred when Mr. W. was at work and George was in the company of his siblings. Mrs. W. reported

Many children with ADD manifest characteristics of the disorder both in school and at home.

that her home had become a prison, protected with locks on all the cabinets to prevent George from rummaging for food.

Most attempts by Mrs. W. to confront George with his inappropriate behavior were met by his swearing and physical aggression. She stated, "He knows if he fights, he will get his way." George's parents described their discipline as consisting of spankings and threats by Mr. W. and reprimands by Mrs. W. When George's deviant behavior would escalate, however, his parents would often give in.

The presence of physical aggression suggests the possibility that a Conduct Disorder may develop. This far more serious problem often does not manifest itself until adolescence.

The use of aggression to punish aggression is an example of modeling inappropriate behavior. When this type of interaction is sustained over time, it can become quite coercive.

Mrs. W. also said that George had few friends and often fought with other children in the neighborhood. Significant problems also occurred at mealtime, while George was dressing, when Mrs. W. was on the telephone, when visitors were in the house, and when George was asked to do homework.

Children with ADD often have social problems.

EXAMPLE 2: JACKY

Jacky was a 10-year-old fourth grader described by her teachers and parents as socially withdrawn, inattentive in school, and generally unhappy. Her parents, Mr. and Mrs. R., divorced for 4 years, reported that Jacky disliked school and claimed that her classmates teased her about being overweight.

Although ADD is more common in boys, girls are also diagnosed as having the disorder.

Jacky's achievement test scores were all below the 50th percentile, but somehow she managed to achieve above-average grades. Even so, Jacky's school progress reports consistently stated that she put forth minimal effort toward her schoolwork. Mr. and Mrs. R. were confused, reporting that Jacky, who appeared mature for her age, presented no disciplinary problems at home and got along well with neighborhood children and adults.

This discrepancy may be accounted for by lenient, sympathetic teachers.

Although many children with ADD are oppositional and defiant, others are very compliant and relate well, especially to adults.

Mr. Q., Jacky's classroom teacher, felt that Jacky required his constant reinforcement and support throughout the school day. He felt that Jacky was just "slow" and didn't want to do her classwork. Because Mr. Q. believed the primary problem was Jacky's lack of motivation, he had been reluctant to refer Jacky for an evaluation. Therefore, she spent all day in the regular educational program.

Sometimes children with ADD are seen as lazy or unmotivated before their real problems are identified.

In the absence of an evaluation and a subsequent Individual Educational Plan (IEP), Mr. Q. made several educational accommodations for Jacky. Because she appeared to need additional time to complete even a minimal amount of work, he placed her in small groups to complete much of her academic work, gave her untimed tests, and reduced her homework assignments. He also placed her desk near his and

Educational accommodations are often the first line of intervention.

Children with ADD seem to process information more slowly than their same-age peers, perhaps due to underarousal in certain parts of the brain.

allowed her to keep an extra set of books at home for homework. Finally, Mr. Q. developed a token reward program for work completed and established special jobs that Jacky could perform, such as delivering messages to the office. Even with these modifications, Mr. Q. felt that Jacky was showing only modest improvement.

Jacky's interview with the school psychologist provided interesting information concerning her self-esteem. In response to a sentence completion questionnaire, Jacky described herself as "ugly and stupid, poor at making friends, worried about school, and wanting to do things better." She further described herself as a "shy, scared, nervous person who avoids talking to other students and answering questions in class and 'freezes' when teased by classmates." Jacky viewed herself as different because of the many "stupid" things she did and because she was somewhat overweight. She was convinced that the other students noticed and ridiculed the flaws she perceived in herself.

Many children with ADD suffer from low self-esteem.

Some children who express these kinds of concerns may receive an additional diagnosis, such as Overanxious Disorder.

A classroom observation by the school psychologist revealed that Jacky was inattentive, distractible, easily frustrated, and in need of immediate gratification for her efforts. An intellectual evaluation indicated that Jacky's strengths included a general fund of knowledge, social

Direct observation of the child in the classroom by someone other than the teacher is often useful in making a diagnosis.

awareness, and abstract reasoning. Her weaknesses were evident when she was required to think through complex problems and when she had to perform speed tasks involving visual processing. The school psychologist described her as "a girl who does not appear to be attending to nor processing the information."

Formal psychological testing helps to provide a complete picture of the whole child.

Jacky lived with her mother and her younger brother, Frank, age 8. Mr. R., who saw Jacky approximately twice a month, was a 42-year-old construction worker with a high school education; Mrs. R., age 38, was a teacher in a local parochial school. Jacky was described by her parents as a "good girl," easy to live with and cooperative and friendly with her brother. Jacky's interests included scouting, soccer, bowling, and singing in the school and church choirs. Mr. and Mrs. R. were very concerned about Jacky's academic and social difficulties and wanted to do what was best for their daughter.

EXAMPLE 3: DENNIS

Dennis, a 15-year-old high school sophomore, was experiencing difficulties with organization, spelling, reading, maintaining attention, tardiness, and truancy. Previous evaluations showed that Dennis had been experiencing chronic diffi-

For adolescents, truancy may be a red flag signaling a possible Conduct Disorder in addition to ADD.

Chronic behavioral problems early in childhood are thought to be

culties in general school adjustment, acquisition of academic skills such as reading and writing, and behavior since at least fifth grade. These evaluations also showed that Dennis's intelligence was within the high average to superior range. His visual-spatial skills were apparently considerably better than his verbal comprehension. Due to these weaknesses in verbal comprehension, Dennis was classified as perceptually impaired, although the school psychologist was attempting to have him reclassified as emotionally disturbed due to his recent truancy.

A classroom observation performed by a psychologist revealed that Dennis had a great deal of difficulty concentrating. He would often attend to classroom details that no one else considered relevant (e.g., a tear in the window shade) or become distracted by minute background activities and noises. He also seemed to concentrate for only short periods of time unless events were of great interest to him. In spite of this, Dennis seemed to understand the overall meaning of the material being presented.

Because of his apparent need for external stimulation, Dennis had trouble in larger groups in school. He appeared to have a lot of energy and to be in motion much of the time, annoying

associated with more serious social problems later in life.

Intelligence does not appear to have any correlation with ADD.

The label "emotionally disturbed" has a number of negative social, political, and economic implications. Furthermore, its use often contributes to the adversarial relationship that sometimes develops between the home and the school.

Adolescents with ADD often choose friends who are younger

or bothering other students. Although he had a strong social network, most observers considered Dennis's friends to be socially undesirable.

Dennis's teachers reported that he would generally complete his classwork carelessly, without thought, planning, or organization. He was consistently observed trying to get classwork done quickly rather than trying to do it well. Dennis's teachers also described his behavior and academic performance as unpredictable, inconsistent, and nonresponsive to corrective feedback.

Dennis's parents, Mr. and Mrs. N., were extremely motivated to help him overcome his school difficulties. Mr. N., age 52, was a high school guidance counselor, and Mrs. N., age 49, was a school nurse. They had always been involved with Dennis's education, although they currently felt that the school was abandoning him. The exasperated teachers and school support systems wanted to move Dennis to an out-of-district placement or send him to night school when he reached 16. This placed the school and the parents at odds.

and less mature, whereas those without the disorder gravitate toward others based on perceived similarity.

"Faster is better" is a motto many children with ADD live by.

Conflicts between parents and the school system over treatment decisions can create significant obstacles to a successful outcome.

The three case examples presented in this first chapter illustrate the diversity of problems children diagnosed with ADD experience and suggest some important defining characteristics of the disorder. The remaining chapters are designed to help classroom teachers meet the challenge of ADD by presenting practical information about the needs and treatment of children and adolescents with

ADD. Specifically, chapter 2 traces the history of the ADD diagnosis, discusses common approaches to treatment, and describes the most commonly held myths about ADD. Chapter 3 discusses three theories of child development, each offering a perspective on how children with ADD are different from their peers. Chapter 4 describes a five-stage model for behavioral assessment, involving problem identification, measurement and functional analysis, matching intervention to student, assessment of intervention strategies, and evaluation of the intervention plan. Chapter 5 discusses specific assessment methods to be used within the context of the five-stage model; the data gathered by such methods help form a comprehensive picture of the child with ADD. Chapter 6 analyzes basic issues that must be addressed before designing an intervention strategy—for example, the teacher's professional role, the need for a directive teaching style, and attentional differences in children with ADD. Chapters 7 and 8 respectively discuss the use of antecedent and consequence interventions to structure the academic environment and encourage appropriate behavior. Chapter 9 outlines the School Environment Learning Program (SELP), a specific consequence intervention for improving classroom performance. Chapter 10 discusses the application of cognitive-behavior therapy to help students with ADD learn to regulate their own behavior. Finally, chapter 11 speculates on future trends in assessment, diagnosis, and intervention. Throughout these chapters, the situations of George, Jacky, and Dennis are reprised to illustrate basic assessment and treatment issues.

2 Understanding ADD

Attention Deficit Disorder, or ADD, is a widespread problem throughout the educational system in the United States. An estimated 3 to 5% of the school-aged population has been diagnosed with ADD (American Psychiatric Association, 1987; Lambert, Sandoval, & Sassone, 1978). The highest levels of ADD are at the elementary level, where occurrence is estimated to be as high as 15 to 20% (Wender, 1975; Yanow, 1973). Although reports of incidence vary, it is safe to say that every teacher must have the information to respond to the needs of children with ADD. Children with ADD present teachers with a special challenge. In order to meet this challenge teachers must first have accurate, up-to-date information about the disorder. This chapter therefore traces the history of the ADD diagnosis, discusses some common treatment approaches, and outlines 19 myths that often interfere with evaluation and treatment.

HISTORY OF THE ADD DIAGNOSIS

Reports of children displaying behaviors now considered characteristic of ADD exist from as long ago as the early 1900s. The labels used for these children, however, have changed as our understanding of the disorder has evolved.

Reports from the early 1900s describe children with the characteristics of what we now call ADD as having a defect in moral control. Between 1900 and 1950, interest in ADD was influenced by studies of aberrant child behavior resulting from an encephalitis epidemic (1917–1918), epilepsy (1938), head injuries (1941), and lead poisoning (1943). Toward the end of this period, the underlying cause of the characteristics we now associate with ADD was assumed to be brain damage.

Between 1950 and 1960, organic dysfunction replaced actual brain damage as the conventional diagnosis. Overactive children were said to be suffering from Minimal Brain Dysfunction, a diagnosis that, although inaccurate, is still common today. The change in terminology at this point did not reflect an increased understanding of the disorder; all the diagnoses at this time suggested that the syndrome stemmed from undetected structural damage within the brain. Despite the lack of empirical evidence for this view, the brain damage theory has lingered for decades in one form or another.

The nomenclature changed again in the late 1960s. The diagnosis of Hyperkinetic Reaction of Childhood emerged to describe children perceived as being overactive, restless, and in constant motion. This became the official diagnosis included in the second edition of the *Diagnostic and Statistical Manual of Mental Disorders* (DSM-II; American Psychiatric Association, 1968).

At this point, hyperactivity was viewed as a behavioral syndrome that could occur as a result of biological difficulties within the child. This development was a dramatic departure from the paradigm positing brain damage as the cause of the child's maladaptive behaviors. An important belief of the scientific community during this period was that excessive activity was temporary and outgrown by puberty.

By the end of the 1970s, hyperactivity was no longer seen as the major characteristic of the syndrome. Rather, impulsivity, short attention span, low frustration tolerance, distractibility, and aggression were considered the more important features. Specifically, research being conducted in Canada by Dr. Virginia Douglas (e.g., Douglas, 1972) began to focus on sustained attention deficits and impulse control problems observed in children. Although the symptom of hyperactivity was observed to diminish in adolescence, difficulties sustaining attention and controlling impulses continued.

By the next decade, the problem of sustained attention was given prominence in the third edition of the *Diagnostic and Statistical Manual* (DSM-III; American Psychiatric Association, 1980). Two distinct diagnoses, Attention Deficit Disorder With Hyperactivity (ADD/+H) and Attention Deficit Disorder Without Hyperactivity (ADD/−H), were identified. The criteria for these two diagnoses are shown in Table 2.1.

Table 2.1   **Diagnostic Criteria for Attention Deficit Disorder With Hyperactivity (ADD/+H) and Attention Deficit Disorder Without Hyperactivity (ADD/−H)**

Attention Deficit Disorder With Hyperactivity

The child displays, for his or her mental and chronological age, signs of developmentally inappropriate inattention, impulsivity, and hyperactivity. The signs must be reported by adults in the child's environment, such as parents and teachers. Because the symptoms are typically variable, they may not be observed directly by the clinician. When the reports of teachers and parents conflict, primary consideration should be given to the teacher reports because of greater familiarity with age-appropriate norms. Symptoms typically worsen in situations that require self-application, as in the classroom. Signs of the disorder may be absent when the child is in a new or one-to-one situation.

The number of symptoms specified is for children between the ages of 8 and 10, the peak age range for referral. In younger children, more severe forms of the symptoms and a greater number of symptoms are usually present. The opposite is true of older children.

A. Inattention. At least three of the following:

 1. Often fails to finish things he or she starts

 2. Often doesn't seem to listen

 3. Easily distracted

 4. Has difficulty concentrating on schoolwork or other tasks requiring sustained attention

 5. Has difficulty sticking to a play activity

B. Impulsivity. At least three of the following:

 1. Often acts before thinking

 2. Shifts excessively from one activity to another

 3. Has difficulty organizing work (this not being due to cognitive impairment)

 4. Needs a lot of supervision

Table 2.1, *continued*

    5. Frequently calls out in class

    6. Has difficulty awaiting turn in games or group situations

C. Hyperactivity. At least two of the following:

    1. Runs about or climbs on things excessively

    2. Has difficulty sitting still or fidgets excessively

    3. Has difficulty staying seated

    4. Moves about excessively during sleep

    5. Is always "on the go" or acts as if "driven by a motor"

D. Onset before the age of 7

E. Duration of at least 6 months

F. Not due to Schizophrenia, Affective Disorder, or Severe or Profound Mental Retardation

Attention Deficit Disorder Without Hyperactivity

The criteria for this disorder are the same as those for Attention Deficit Disorder with Hyperactivity except that the individual never had signs of hyperactivity (Criterion C).

From *Diagnostic and Statistical Manual of Mental Disorders* (3rd ed., pp. 43–44) by the American Psychiatric Association, 1980, Washington, DC: Author. Copyright 1980 by the American Psychiatric Association. Reprinted by permission.

    Due to the lack of empirical data regarding ADD/−H, the revised third edition of the *Diagnostic and Statistical Manual* (DSM-III-R; American Psychiatric Association, 1987) combined ADD/+H and ADD/−H as Attention Deficit Hyperactivity Disorder (ADHD).

    The current criteria for this diagnosis are shown in Table 2.2. To satisfy scientists and clinicians who questioned this decision, the diagnosis of Undifferentiated Attention Deficit Disorder (UADD) was added, with a disclaimer noting that further research would be necessary to determine its validity. In UADD, signs of impulsiveness and hyperactivity are not present.

Table 2.2   Diagnostic Criteria for Attention Deficit Hyperactivity Disorder (ADHD)

Note: Consider a criterion met only if the behavior is considerably more frequent than that of most people of the same mental age.

A. A disturbance of at least 6 months during which at least eight of the following are present:

1. Often fidgets with hands or feet or squirms in seat (in adolescents, may be limited to subjective feelings of restlessness)

2. Has difficulty remaining seated when required to do so

3. Is easily distracted by extraneous stimuli

4. Has difficulty awaiting turn in games or group situations

5. Often blurts out answers to questions before they have been completed

6. Has difficulty following through on instructions from others (not due to oppositional behavior or failure of comprehension), e.g., fails to finish chores

7. Has difficulty sustaining attention in tasks or play activities

8. Often shifts from one uncompleted activity to another

9. Has difficulty playing quietly

10. Often talks excessively

11. Often interrupts or intrudes on others, e.g., butts into other children's games

12. Often does not seem to listen to what is being said to him or her

13. Often loses things necessary for tasks or activities at school or at home, e.g., toys, pencils, books, assignments

14. Often engages in physically dangerous activities without considering possible consequences (not for purpose of thrill-seeking), e.g., runs into street without looking

Note: The above items are listed in descending order of discriminating power based on data from a national field trial of the DSM-III-R criteria for Disruptive Behavior Disorders.

Table 2.2, *continued*

B. Onset before the age of 7

C. Does not meet the criteria for a Pervasive Developmental Disorder

Criteria for severity of Attention Deficit Hyperactivity Disorder:

Mild: Few, if any, symptoms in excess of those required to make the diagnosis and only minimal or no impairment in school and social functioning

Moderate: Symptoms or functional impairment between "mild" *and* "severe"

Severe: Many symptoms in excess of those required to make the diagnosis *and* significant and pervasive impairment in functioning at home and school and with peers

---

From *Diagnostic and Statistical Manual of Mental Disorders* (3rd ed. rev., pp. 52–53) by the American Psychiatric Association, 1987, Washington, DC: Author. Copyright 1987 by the American Psychiatric Association. Reprinted by permission.

The fourth edition of the *Diagnostic and Statistical Manual* (DSM-IV), expected to be released in 1994, will once again provide two distinct categories of ADD, one with and one without hyperactivity (Task Force on DSM-IV, 1991). Three specific types of diagnoses will be possible: predominantly inattentive, predominantly hyperactive-impulsive, and a combined type. The most current criteria are presented in Table 2.3.

It appears, then, that the diagnostic terminology referring to the behaviors these children display has evolved and will continue to do so as scientists and clinicians develop a better understanding of the disorder.

Table 2.3 DSM-IV Draft Criteria for Attention Deficit Hyperactivity Disorder (ADHD)

A. Either 1 or 2:

1. Inattention: At least six of the following symptoms of inattention have persisted for at least 6 months to a degree that is maladaptive and inconsistent with developmental level:

   a. Often fails to give close attention to details or makes careless mistakes in schoolwork, work, or other activities

   b. Often has difficulty sustaining attention in tasks or play activities

   c. Often does not seem to listen to what is being said to him or her

   d. Often does not follow through on instructions and fails to finish schoolwork, chores, or duties in the work place (not due to oppositional behavior or failure to understand instructions)

   e. Often has difficulties organizing tasks and activities

   f. Often avoids or strongly dislikes tasks (such as schoolwork or homework) that require sustained mental effort

   g. Often loses things necessary for tasks or activities (e.g., school assignments, pencils, books, tools, or toys)

   h. Is often easily distracted by extraneous stimuli

   i. Often forgetful in daily activities

2. Hyperactivity-Impulsivity: At least six of the following symptoms of hyperactivity-impulsivity have persisted for at least 6 months to a degree that is maladaptive and inconsistent with developmental level:

   HYPERACTIVITY:

   a. Often fidgets with hands or feet or squirms in seat

   b. Leaves seat in classroom or in other situations in which remaining seated is expected

Table 2.3, *continued*

    c. Often runs about or climbs excessively in situations where it is inappropriate (in adolescents or adults, may be limited to subjective feelings of restlessness)

    d. Often has difficulty playing or engaging in leisure activities quietly

    e. Often talks excessively

    f. Often acts as if "driven by a motor" and cannot remain still

IMPULSIVITY:

    g. Often blurts out answers to questions before the questions have been completed

    h. Often has difficulty waiting in lines or awaiting turn in games or group situations

    i. Often interrupts or intrudes on others

B. Onset no later than 7 years of age.

C. Symptoms must be present in two or more situations (e.g., at school, work, and at home)

D. The disturbance causes clinically significant distress or impairment in social, academic, or occupational functioning

E. Does not occur exclusively during the course of a Pervasive Developmental Disorder, Schizophrenia, or other Psychotic Disorder, and is not better accounted for by a Mood Disorder, Anxiety Disorder, Dissociative Disorder, or Personality Disorder

---

From *DSM-IV Draft Criteria: 3/1/93* by the American Psychiatric Association, 1993, Washington, DC: Author. Copyright 1993 by the American Psychiatric Association. Reprinted by permission.

COMMON APPROACHES TO TREATMENT

As new knowledge led to changes in the diagnostic labeling of children with ADD, so too did it lead to new treatment theories. The most commonly used interventions for children with ADD from the mid-1960s until the present are behavior therapy, cognitive-behavior therapy, and stimulant medication.

Behavior Therapy

Behavior therapy has been a cornerstone of intervention with the ADD population since the mid-1960s. During that period, case studies on hyperactive children began to appear in the literature. Clinicians working with these children commonly used social learning approaches. Such approaches involved training parents, on a short-term basis, in the use of praise, ignoring, and punishment procedures such as time-out. Classroom teachers were also trained in these techniques as well as in the use of token reinforcement programs. These programs identified specific target behaviors, assigned them point values, and made use of a system of rewards and privileges to encourage children to respond more appropriately. (Chapter 8, on consequence interventions, and chapter 9, on the School Environment Learning Program, describe interventions based on the assumptions of social learning theory.)

Considered the first generation of behavior therapy, these early approaches did obtain positive results. Treatments were typically very short and tended to omit long-term follow-up. Thus, this first generation of therapy seemed to concentrate on developing techniques and demonstrating that change could occur.

However, children with ADD are in need of consistent interventions maintained over an extended period of time. When these early interventions were discontinued, it was common to observe maladaptive or inappropriate behaviors reverting to their previous levels. This problem was identified by behavior therapists as the failure of the interventions to generalize outside the initial treatment settings.

Cognitive-Behavior Therapy

Some critics of early behavioral approaches perceived the crux of the generalization problem as a lack of the child's active involvement. In order to rectify this problem, behavior therapy expanded to include the child as his or her own agent of change. This process, developed in the 1970s, came to be known as cognitive-behavior therapy, or CBT. CBT incorporates the idea of "private speech" or "self-talk" into interventions. This process helps the child to generalize gains made in training independently of the responses of external agents such as parents or teachers. (For a more detailed discussion of how CBT works, see chapter 10.)

It was during the 1980s that CBT matured as an intervention. Although the approach is relatively new, there has been an ongoing controversy as to its effectiveness. Many believe that cognitive interventions are simply not powerful enough to override a faulty social learning environment in which inappropriate behaviors are reinforced and appropriate behaviors are not. Although CBT was originally developed in order to provide the cognitive tools that would make children less dependent on the environment, it is becoming obvious that children with ADD need persistent prompting over a long period of time to incorporate any cognitive strategies.

Stimulant Medications

Much like insulin for persons with diabetes or prescription eyeglasses for persons with myopia, stimulant medications for children with ADD are a cornerstone of a comprehensive treatment program. Stimulant medications have proven to be the most robust form of intervention available, and the classroom teacher occupies a unique role in their overall use.

Stimulant medications are believed to affect certain neurotransmitter chemicals (e.g., norepinephrine) in areas of the brain primarily responsible for the ability to pay attention and to inhibit motor responding (Copeland, 1991). The most widely used stimulant medication is Ritalin (generic name, methylphenidate), with Dexedrine (dextroamphetamine) and Cylert (pemoline) being used secondarily. This general class of medications has been used for over 50 years in the treatment of disruptive behavior disorders in children (Bradley, 1937). Ritalin has been used in the treatment of children with hyperactivity since the mid-1950s. By the 1970s Ritalin was in widespread use. During the following decade, many abuses of this medication took place as a result of its being prescribed for behavior control without careful assessment and diagnosis. These abuses contributed to a backlash in which teachers, parents, and professionals cautioned against its use. Further study has resulted in more rigorous application and the abatement of these types of abuses. By the 1980s the effects of stimulant medication on social behavior and mental ability began to be considered separately. Currently, intervention for children with ADD would not be considered complete without a serious trial of stimulant medication.

Stimulant medications have a broad impact: First, since they enhance those parts of the central nervous system responsible for the ability to pay attention, concentrate, and inhibit impulsivity, a child may appear calmer and more relaxed physiologically. (Because of this effect, a common misconception about stimulant medications is that they are tranquilizers.) Second, a positive response can often be seen behaviorally. In other words, children often show improvements in direction following and self-directed behavior. In the classroom, they are less likely to be defiant. Third, such medications appear to be related to increased social acceptance, as seen in sociometric ratings. Finally, they may enhance a child's academic functioning, with children being more likely to complete both classwork and homework. The classroom teacher will often notice improvement in handwriting and greater persistence of effort in tasks considered arduous or boring.

Approximately 70 to 80% of all children with ADD will show a positive response to stimulant medications (Copeland, 1991). Although this percentage is significant, it means that some children will not show a positive response, or, if they do, results will be attenuated by adverse side effects. The most common adverse side effects are decreased appetite and sleep disturbances. Other adverse effects, reported with less frequency, are stomachaches, headaches, irritability, and tics. Concern has also been expressed about the long-term use of stimulant medications and effects on height, weight, heart rate, and blood pressure (Safer & Allen, 1973).

When stimulant medications have not been effective, other medications have been used, in many cases with positive results. The most commonly used second-line medications are tricyclic antidepressants (i.e., imipramine and desipramine). These medications operate differently from stimulant medications in that they take longer to reach a therapeutic level in the bloodstream. Because these medications are longer acting, they do not need to be administered as frequently as do stimulant medications, but because they can affect heart conduction, they need to be more closely monitored. At times, stimulant medication may be combined with tricyclic antidepressant medication, but this is typically done only under the close supervision of a physician. (For a more detailed account of the use of various medications with this population, the reader is referred to Copeland, 1991).

The classroom teacher occupies a central role in administering and monitoring the use of medications. First, the effects of a stimulant medication such as Ritalin may peak within 1½ to 2 hours after administration, and the medication may no longer be effective after 3 to 5 hours. Because the medication may need to be readministered by the school nurse around lunchtime, the child's interpersonal sensitivity needs to be considered. A teacher may inadvertently stigmatize a child by publicly announcing that it is time to visit the nurse or by questioning the child after the display of inappropriate classroom behavior as to whether the child remembered to take his or her "pill." Any discussion of medication should be done in private and with utmost concern for the child's feelings. The classroom teacher will also need to be alert to the possibility that the need for medication may result in other students' targeting the child with ADD for ridicule. Finally, some children resist going to the nurse because they do not want to be singled out and appear different from their peers. Under some conditions it is useful to provide further education about the role of medication, address the negative reactions of other students, or explore the possible use of a longer acting medication that may obviate the need for a midday administration.

Second, because the prescribing physician, mental health professional, and parents cannot be present in the school setting, the classroom teacher is often solely responsible for monitoring the effects of medication. The teacher's feedback is therefore critical to the success of a treatment plan. The teacher may share anecdotal information about the child's behavior, academic performance, and mood in handwritten notes or in direct conversation. Because this type of information may be biased, behavior rating scales are also helpful. The scale most commonly used for this purpose is the Conners' Abbreviated Teacher Rating Scale (CATRS; Goyette, Conners, & Ulrich, 1978), a 10-item checklist that asks the classroom teacher to rate various behaviors on a four-point scale. This rating scale can be completed by one or more teachers on a daily basis. The scores allow for a more objective measure of the child's responsiveness to medication.

NINETEEN MYTHS ABOUT ADD

In an attempt to understand ADD, teachers must sort their way through a series of inaccuracies, misconceptions, and misunderstandings. For nearly a hundred years, myths concerning the source and scope of ADD have frustrated efforts to address behavioral problems in the classroom. Whenever classroom interventions for children with ADD are based on myths or false assumptions, they will fail. Only by "demythifying" ADD, by probing its true nature, will teachers' efforts succeed.

Myth 1: ADD is a new psychological disorder

As already discussed, beginning about 1900, reports in medical journals identified children who exhibited impaired attention and who were described as seriously overactive. Although the diagnostic labels have varied widely, the behaviors that have inspired them are certainly not new.

Myth 2: ADD is occurring in epidemic proportions

The amount of press coverage that ADD has received in recent years has caused a good deal of confusion and controversy regarding the disorder. Not a week goes by without a magazine or newspaper article about ADD. Some authors have discussed reasons for a possible increase in ADD. One suggestion is that improved medical techniques allow for the survival of high-risk infants who are likely to show signs of ADD within a few years. Critics of this view do not believe that ADD has actually increased at all, saying rather that our ability to diagnosis the disorder has improved. In fact, the percentage of the population either diagnosed or at risk for ADD has not varied considerably since the early 1900s, when ADD as a disorder was first identified. Roughly 3 to 5% of the population is affected (American Psychiatric Association, 1987). What is true is that the public is increasingly aware of the disorder and is predisposed to cite it as an explanation for why children are failing academically, behaviorally, and socially.

Myth 3: ADD is only the latest diagnostic fad and will be replaced by another disorder in the near future

Clearly, ADD is not a diagnostic fad; rather, it is an area of difficulty that has been with us for a long time and will be with us for a long time to come. However, the educational mandate to provide special services for children as young as age 3 has increased the likelihood that children who display difficulties in this setting will be identified.

Myth 4: Hyperactivity is the primary component of ADD

Researchers and clinicians currently debate whether inattention and impulsivity, on the one hand, or hyperactivity, on the other, is the most significant component of ADD. As discussed previously, the diagnoses ADD/+H and ADD/−H were dropped in the DSM-III-R because of a consensus that inattention, impulsivity, and hyperactivity generally occur together. Therefore, ADD/+H became the predominant view. This approach deemphasized a child's difficulties with attention deployment (e.g., remaining on task) and response inhibition (e.g., reacting to environmental stimuli) and emphasized the degree of overactivity.

Hyperactivity does cross various behavioral domains and often causes a child to be labeled as deviant in social as well as academic settings: For example, George was described by his third-grade teacher as being unable to stay in his seat or keep his hands off his fellow students. For teachers, a student's hyperactivity can cause significant social and behavioral problems for the remainder of the class. However, it is important to understand that children do not have to be hyperactive to have ADD. Inattention and impulsivity also affect a child's everyday life, including academic functioning and self-control. Even in the absence of hyperactivity, such deficits can cause problems throughout an individual's academic and social life.

Myth 5: ADD is the result of an overactive brain

Although the exact mechanism is unknown, current research indicates that ADD is neurobiologically based. In other words, the attention deficits, high activity levels, and impulsivity associated with ADD can best be described in terms of neurochemical actions within the brain.

Despite the prevailing myth, ADD appears to be the result of an underactive, not overactive, brain. The work of Dr. Alan Zametkin (1990) supports this notion: Zametkin used a brain mapping technique called Positron Emission Tomography (PET) to measure glucose metabolism in the brain. Glucose has a significant effect on the level of neurological activity, and the PET scan can actually provide a picture of the brain's metabolic activity. Using PET scans, Zametkin assessed brain activity in adults diagnosed with ADD who were the biological parents of children who also had this disorder, comparing these adults' brain activity with that of a group of adults without ADD. Participants were asked to perform mental tasks involving attention, concentration, and inhibition of motor responding. Zametkin found that those areas of the brain responsible for attention, concentration, and inhibition of motor responding were actually less active (i.e., underaroused) in the ADD group. His findings underscored the neurobiological basis for ADD and suggested that underarousal in the brain and insufficient central nervous system inhibition are the causative cornerstones of ADD.

In other words, in ADD the understimulation of the child's brain creates a motivation for external stimulation. Increased activity, distractibility, and difficulties with impulse control may be explained as a child's attempts to cope with boredom due to low levels of external stimulation. Through the use of stimulant medication such as Ritalin, which increases the brain's activity level and thereby lessens the need for external stimulation, a child's activity rate and distractibility may be reduced.

Myth 6: Children with ADD demonstrate the same behaviors in all settings

As parents can attest, a child diagnosed as having ADD does not always display the same behaviors in all situations. When viewing the behaviors of children with ADD, we must consider two competing variables: setting demands and task complexity. Variations in setting and task demands often explain the reason children with ADD demonstrate inconsistent behavior.

Setting demands—the degree of structure imposed in a situation—can have a significant effect on behavior. When the setting is highly structured, children with ADD may appear identical to their peers without ADD. This explains why most of these children's behavioral difficulties occur during unstructured activities such as recess, lunch, and special school events. If classroom teachers impose the right kind of structure, children with ADD can be helped to overcome the inability to regulate their own behavior.

As *task complexity* increases, so does the probability that performance will deteriorate. Difficulties with problem solving, planning, and organization exacerbate deficiencies in self-regulation. In presenting classroom material, then, the teacher must be mindful of the level of complexity at which a child with ADD demonstrates a decline in performance.

Myth 7: Children with ADD demonstrate the same behaviors with all adults

Because the performance of children with ADD is contingent on setting demands and task complexity, it is not surprising to find that these children perform better with an adult within close proximity. The presence of this adult can be seen as an external stimulus that decreases problem behaviors. But children with ADD can demonstrate vastly different degrees of self-control when in the presence of different adults.

One issue of particular concern is the varied degree of compliant and disruptive behavior children with ADD will display with mothers and fathers. In spite of social changes in family roles, for the most part mothers are still the primary custodians of children. Typically, during the course of a day mothers find themselves responsible for supervising their children's personal hygiene, daily chores, contact with the community, and homework. Because of the large amount of time spent and the nature of the activities supervised, mothers are likely targets for their children's behavioral difficulties. In general, fathers have comparatively less contact with their children. As a result, they are more novel; they also tend to talk less and punish more, have deeper voices, and be physically stronger. These factors may all contribute to their achieving greater compliance.

Teachers' roles are also different. As children with ADD move through the educational system, they meet different personalities. The result is that these children may function well one year and not so well the next. A teacher's behavioral management style plays an important part in controlling the intensity and frequency of behavior problems. A high degree of consistency and the provision of structure and task demands within the child's ability improve the likelihood that the child will succeed. Also, if the classroom teacher can refocus the child without entering into a power struggle—that is, without being threatened by the child's perceived intransigence—behavioral difficulties can be decreased.

Many adults—both teachers and parents—tend to set unrealistic expectations that increase the likelihood of failure. At times, children with ADD will rise to the challenge and succeed, but at other times they will fail. Whether due to changes in the adult, the situation, the task, or some unknown variable, behavioral inconsistency is now seen as a core characteristic of ADD.

Myth 8: Girls can't have ADD

Girls can and do have ADD, although research indicates significant differences in the incidence of ADD among males and females. The ratio of boys to girls with ADD ranges from 4:1 to 10:1, with 6:1 being the generally accepted bench mark (Ross & Ross, 1982). Some authors hypothesize that because girls with ADD are less likely to be aggressive, oppositional, or antisocial—and/or to display overt behavioral problems—they are less likely to be identified in school or home settings. In general, girls display fewer conduct problems than boys; therefore, they are not referred for educational or psychological evaluations at the same rate. Further research is needed in this area to improve the detection and treatment of girls diagnosed with ADD.

Myth 9: All children with ADD have learning disabilities

Learning disabilities are significantly associated with ADD, but not all children with ADD have learning disabilities. The incidence of learning disabilities in the school-age population is estimated at 10%; however, if a child is diagnosed with ADD, the probability that he or she has a learning disability jumps to roughly 30% (Barkley, 1990). Children with ADD often experience academic problems in at least one area, such as math, reading, spelling, or handwriting.

The best indicator of a learning disability is the failure of a child to do work assigned in school. However, underachievement is not considered a statistically significant problem if no notable discrepancy exists between the child's intelligence or mental capacity and academic performance. Generally, school systems will not initiate an evaluation unless a child is performing two grades below current grade level. However, even if a child with ADD does not have a specific learning disability, teachers will need to consider making academic accommodations to address behavioral problems. Procedures such as checking the student's understanding of an assignment before actually beginning work and on completion, pairing the student with a peer tutor or social buddy, and the like can help the student achieve to the greatest possible degree.

Myth 10: Children with ADD are emotionally disturbed

The inconsistency that characterizes ADD has led some people to conclude that children with ADD are emotionally disturbed. Teachers may ask, "Why is this child fine during physical education, but when he gets into social studies all hell breaks loose?" or "Why can she spend hours at the computer but not complete a single spelling assignment?"

The view that emotional disturbances are caused by ADD is problematic. Research in the area of ADD and emotional disturbance is inconsistent. Some studies suggest that children with ADD have a greater propensity for anxiety, depression, and low self-esteem when compared with same-age peers without difficulties or even same-age peers with learning disabilities (e.g., Breen & Barkley, 1983; Weiss & Hechtman, 1986). Other studies have found no greater incidence of any disorder in children with ADD (e.g., Barkley, DuPaul, & McMurray, 1990).

The symptoms that characterize ADD do not in themselves imply emotional disturbance. However, educators must keep in mind that these children face enormous challenges due to their ADD symptoms. If children with ADD do not get help, their behavioral problems may take on far greater weight and can foster emotional difficulties. When ADD does underlie emotional problems, the ADD symptoms must be addressed directly.

Myth 11: Children with ADD are found equally in all socioeconomic groups

Although children with ADD come from all walks of life, a higher proportion of children with ADD come from lower socioeconomic backgrounds (Barkley, 1990; Trites, 1979). Two reasons are suggested for these findings: First, poor prenatal care received by mothers in lower socioeconomic groups may affect the development of the fetal brain, thus increasing the risk of ADD. Second, parents from lower socioeconomic groups may have a greater incidence of ADD themselves, suggesting a genetic component that researchers have not thus far identified.

Myth 12: Faulty parenting causes ADD

Some theories of ADD have been interpreted to suggest that poor parenting is the underlying cause of the disorder. For example, social learning theory might be seen to support the notion that childhood behavior problems are the result of a faulty learning environment in which reinforcements are too infrequent to support the learning of appropriate behavior. (See chapter 3 for more about social learning theory.) However, most evidence suggests that parental stress, depression, and other psychological difficulties are the *result* rather than the *cause* of a child's ADD.

It is important to note, however, that the problems of children with ADD can be so challenging and aversive that parents do occasionally respond inappropriately—for instance, by yelling or becoming coercive. A coercive approach involving the use of aversive techniques to handle opposition, defiance, and excessive behavior can make children's already existing problems even worse. The best way to counteract the effects of a coercive pattern is to master the behavior management skills required to address the needs of the child with ADD. Families with more than one child illustrate the need for parents to learn different approaches: The siblings of a child with ADD may have little problem negotiating their environment, and the parents can use low-level management approaches with them. But the same approaches are clearly inadequate to address the needs of the child with ADD.

Myth 13: Diet and nutrition play a major role in the development of ADD and its treatment

In the 1970s, diet and nutrition were believed to play a major role in a wide variety of behavior disorders of childhood. The current research suggests no support for treatments that control diet and nutrition (Conners, 1980). Most studies have concluded that, at most, 10% of children with ADD show mild increases in symptoms as a result of food additives (Barkley, 1981; Ross & Ross, 1982). These children tend to be younger than 6 years of age and have displayed a history of responding to diet as evaluated by subjective parent report.

Sugar has often been cited as exacerbating ADD behavior, but recent research indicates there is no relationship between sugar intake and ADD (e.g., Milich & Pelham, 1986; Whalen & Henker, 1980). Generally, when children are given sugary foods, it is at a time when their excessive behavior is permitted, such as at parties or during the lunch hour. When these children return to a more sedate situation, such as a classroom, they frequently have difficulty controlling the behavior that had been tolerated previously in the alternate setting.

Myth 14: Preschool children are the easiest population to diagnose with ADD

Developmental level plays a big part in the ease of diagnosing ADD. Preschool children are actually the most difficult group to diagnose. Inattention, impulsivity, and overactivity are common in young children, although these tendencies are outgrown with age. In addition, task demands on young children (e.g., sitting quietly at a desk) are few, so behavior associated with ADD may not yet be apparent. Finally, young children may not be exposed to formal observations that would detect ADD symptoms.

Some very general criteria for diagnosing ADD in children of various ages are as follows: for children ages 4 through 6, ten symptoms; for children ages 7 through 9, eight symptoms; and for children age 10 and over, six symptoms (see Table 2.2). The symptom picture does change over time, and it is important to identify children as early as possible.

Myth 15: ADD is a time-limited disorder, and children will grow out of it on their own as they get older

It is true that activity level does tend to decline in adolescence and that attention span and impulse control tend to improve. Thus, ADD may not seem as acute as during the early years. However, children do not simply outgrow ADD. Research indicates that anywhere from 25 to 35% of children receiving an initial diagnosis of ADD are diagnosed during adolescence as antisocial or conduct disordered, continuing to display behaviors that cause them to fail in academic endeavors, social relationships, and emotional growth (Brown & Borden, 1986).

In some cases, these difficulties and symptoms continue unabated throughout adolescence and into young adulthood. Clinicians are seeing more and more adults who continue to display inattention and impulsivity and who are in need of ongoing assistance. Estimates suggest that 50 to 65% of children with ADD will show significant impairment in adulthood with regard to employment, interpersonal relationships, and/or emotional well-being (Weiss & Hechtman, 1986). These adults generally demonstrate lower academic achievement and are of lower socioeconomic status than their peers who do not have ADD. Problems with antisocial behaviors may continue to be troublesome for 20 to 45% of these adults, although approximately 25% may meet the criteria for a diagnosis of Antisocial Personality Disorder (Barkley, 1990). Adults with ADD have also been found to have a higher likelihood of substance abuse than their peers without ADD. It should be noted, however, that a majority of individuals with this disorder are able to make significant adjustments to these problem areas in adulthood.

Myth 16: If ADD is identified early enough, it can be cured

As just discussed, children do not outgrow ADD. Nor is there a cure for this lifelong disorder. Treatment combining stimulant medication, educational accommodations, behavioral training for parents, family counseling, and individual counseling as children become older can improve the prognosis, however. Although such treatment is not a cure, it does provide children with healthy compensatory strategies to help them contend with a world that is sometimes insensitive to their problems. The School Environment Learning Program (SELP), outlined in chapter 9, attempts to teach such skills. Other programs with similar intent include Social Problem Solving (Clabby & Elias, 1986), Think Aloud (Camp & Bash, 1981), and Stop and Think (Kendall, 1988). As is the case for other psychological or developmental disorders, the earlier treatment is begun, the better.

It is important to help parents understand that treatment will need to extend over a long period of time and to discuss with them a plan that covers the child's entire schooling. A central component of this plan is the parents' understanding that ADD does not go away, although the severity of the behavioral problems will fluctuate. Parents must also recognize that as setting demands increase, the symptoms of ADD will increase. Troublesome periods are generally in the first grade, when a child is first required to sit at a desk, complete classwork, and do homework; fourth grade, at which point educational requirements and task demands increase dramatically; seventh grade, when most school systems become departmentalized and children are required to interact with up to six different teachers; and high school, when the larger environment may be intimidating and confusing, causing children with specific difficulties to feel overwhelmed and lost. To put this long-term plan into effect, parents and teachers need to be aware of the complexities of ADD and the accommodations required to help these children function at each step along the educational and developmental continuum.

Myth 17: There is no way to predict how a child with ADD will do in adolescence or adulthood

No single predictor foretells the outcome for a specific child with ADD. However, a combination of factors may provide a window to the future. Variables such as family support, socioeconomic status, and level of intelligence, as well as the nature and timing of a multimodal intervention, bear upon emotional, academic, social, and behavioral adjustment during adolescence. Close observation of a child's behavior, in combination with an understanding of environmental factors, allows the formation of a reasonable opinion about the outcome of this disorder in adolescence and adulthood.

Specifically, studies have found that socioeconomic status does play a role in the development of adolescents with ADD. Families of lower socioeconomic status appear to have more severe problems with adolescents diagnosed as having ADD, and these children appear to have more significant pathology (Barkley, 1990). Although socioeconomic status has not been found to be a strong predictor of outcome at adolescence or adulthood, it is considered to play a part along with other factors (Weiss & Hechtman, 1986). General level of intelligence also correlates with eventual academic achievement and occupational success. Children who have good social skills and hence have positive relationships with their peers are more likely to be interpersonally successful, experiencing fewer pathological difficulties later on in life (Guevremont, 1990; Weiss & Hechtman, 1986). Aggression and conduct problems during childhood and adolescence, on the other hand, suggest a more negative prognosis for adjustment in adulthood (Barkley, 1990; Weiss & Hechtman, 1986). Parental psychopathology also increases the risk of other psychiatric problems of adolescence and early adulthood, such as depression, anxiety, and low self-esteem, as well as more severe problems such as personality disorders (Weiss & Hechtman, 1986).

Myth 18: Stimulant medication is limited in its effectiveness to children with ADD

It was once believed that a positive response to stimulant medication could be used to confirm a diagnosis of ADD. It is now accepted that responsiveness to stimulant medication cannot be used to diagnose this disorder because many people without ADD show marked improvement when medicated. Because studies show that stimulant medication has across-the-board success—that is, it improves the behavior of all individuals whether or not they have ADD—the use of such medication in diagnosis should have been invalidated years ago. But, as is often the case with ADD, the myth continues to be widespread.

Another erroneous belief is that stimulant medication, although effective in 75 to 80% of all cases in childhood, is not effective in adolescence and adulthood. The current literature now indicates that stimulant medication may be quite useful in treating adolescents and adults with ADD. Several studies have found positive results with both stimulant and antidepressant medications. Adults who take stimulant medication have demonstrated decreased nervousness, improvement in concentration, and better impulse control.

Myth 19: Children with ADD are ineligible for special education services

Children with ADD do qualify for special education services if there is evidence of impairment as a result of the condition. A recent clarification by the Office of Education, citing Public Law 94–142 as well as Section 504 of the Rehabilitation Act, requires public schools to make necessary educational accommodations to provide a free and appropriate public education for children who, as a result of ADD, present with problems in alertness (i.e., attention). Children with ADD can also receive special education services if it is determined that they have other problems for which special education services are mandated (e.g., perceptual impairment, neurological impairment, behavior disorder).

If a child receives a diagnosis other than ADD, he or she will likely be schooled in classes for children with similar problems (i.e., learning disabilities or behavior disorders). It is vital to consider the nature and degree of difficulty the child is experiencing. If the child is oppositional and has conduct problems such as aggression, the most likely placement will be in a class for emotionally or behaviorally disturbed children. If behavioral difficulties are minimal and learning difficulties are prominent, the child may be placed in a class for perceptually or neurologically impaired students or receive resource room services.

The views of school system personnel, who are required to provide the least restrictive educational setting, may at times be at odds with those of teachers or parents. Teachers may not feel able to adjust their classroom structure or task demands to accommodate a child with ADD. Parents may want their child to be placed in a class with a lower teacher-to-student ratio that allows for more individualized attention, or they may not want their child labeled and thus refuse special services altogether.

The varying manifestations of ADD mean that no single educational option will work for all children. With greater understanding of the individual child's problem, a school system can better focus interventions on the academic, behavioral, social, and emotional domains affected by this disorder.

References

American Psychiatric Association. (1968). *Diagnostic and statistical manual of mental disorders* (2nd ed.). Washington, DC: Author.

American Psychiatric Association. (1980). *Diagnostic and statistical manual of mental disorders* (3rd ed.). Washington, DC: Author.

American Psychiatric Association. (1987). *Diagnostic and statistical manual of mental disorders* (3rd ed. rev.). Washington, DC: Author.

American Psychiatric Association. (1993). *DSM-IV draft criteria: 3/1/93.* Washington, DC: Author.

Barkley, R. A. (1981). *Hyperactive children: A handbook for diagnosis and treatment.* New York: Guilford.

Barkley, R. A. (1990). *Attention Deficit Hyperactivity Disorder: A handbook for diagnosis and treatment.* New York: Guilford.

Barkley, R. A., DuPaul, G. J., & McMurray, M. B. (1990). A comprehensive evaluation of Attention Deficit Disorder With and Without Hyperactivity defined by research criteria. *Journal of Consulting and Clinical Psychology, 58,* 775–789.

Bradley, W. (1937). The behavior of children receiving benzedrine. *American Journal of Psychiatry, 94,* 577–585.

Breen, M. J., & Barkley, R. A. (1983). The Personality Inventory for Children: Its clinical utility with hyperactive children. *Journal of Pediatric Psychology, 8,* 359–366.

Brown, R. T., & Borden, K. A. (1986). Hyperactivity at adolescence: Some misconceptions and new directions. *Journal of Clinical Child Psychology, 15,* 194–209.

Camp, B. W., & Bash, M. A. S. (1981). *Think Aloud: Increasing social and cognitive skills—A problem-solving program for children.* Champaign, IL: Research Press.

Clabby, J. F., & Elias, M. J. (1986). *Teach your child decision making.* New York: Doubleday.

Conners, C. K. (1980). *Food additives and hyperactive children.* New York: Plenum.

Copeland, E. D. (1991). *Medication for attention disorders (ADHD/ADD) and related medical problems (Tourette's Syndrome, sleep apnea, seizure disorder): A comprehensive handbook.* Atlanta, GA: SPI.

Douglas, V. I. (1972). Stop, look, and listen: The problem of sustained attention and impulse control in hyperactive and normal children. *Canadian Journal of Behavioral Science, 4,* 259–282.

Goyette, C. H., Conners, C. K., & Ulrich, R. F. (1978). Normative data on revised Conners' Parent and Teacher Rating Scales. *Journal of Abnormal Child Psychology, 6,* 221–236.

Guevremont, D. (1990). Social skills and peer relationship training. In R. A. Barkley (Ed.), *Attention deficit hyperactivity disorder: A handbook for diagnosis and treatment* (pp. 540–572). New York: Guilford.

Kendall, P. C. (1988). *Stop and Think workbook.* Unpublished manuscript, Temple University, Philadelphia.

Lambert, N. M., Sandoval, J., & Sassone, D. (1978). Prevalence of hyperactivity in elementary school children as a function of the social system definers. *American Journal of Orthopsychiatry, 48,* 446–463.

Milich, R., & Pelham, W. E. (1986). Effects of sugar ingestion on the classroom and playgroup behavior of Attention Deficit Disorder boys. *Journal of Consulting and Clinical Psychology, 54,* 714–718.

Ross, D. M., & Ross, S. A. (1982). *Hyperactivity: Research, theory, and action* (2nd ed.). New York: Wiley.

Safer, D. J., & Allen, R. P. (1973). Factors influencing the suppressant effects of two stimulant drugs on the growth of hyperactive children. *Pediatrics, 51,* 660–667.

Task Force on DSM-IV. (1991). *DSM-IV options book: Work in progress: 9/1/91.* Washington, DC: American Psychiatric Press.

Trites, R. L. (1979). *Hyperactivity in children: Etiology, measurement, and treatment implications.* Baltimore: University Park Press.

Weiss, G., & Hechtman, L. (1986). *Hyperactive children grown-up.* New York: Guilford.

Wender, P. H. (1975). The minimal brain dysfunction syndrome. *Annual Review of Medicine, 26,* 45–62.

Whalen, C. K., & Henker, B. (1980). The social ecology of psychostimulant treatment: A model for conceptual and empirical analysis. In C. K. Whalen & B. Henker (Eds.), *Hyperactive children: The social ecology of identification and treatment* (pp. 3–51). New York: Academic.

Yanow, M. (1973). A report on the use of behavior modification drugs on elementary school children. In M. Yanow (Ed.), *Observations from the treadmill* (pp. 85–105). New York: Viking.

Zametkin, A. (1990). Cerebral glucose metabolism in adults with hyperactivity of childhood onset. *New England Journal of Medicine, 323,* 1361, 1366.

3   Child Development Through the ADD Looking Glass: Three Theories

When teachers consider any child's problem behavior, they ask a host of questions, including "How does this behavior compare to the norm?" This chapter briefly discusses three theoretical models of children's cognitive and social development, applying these theories to the specific problems of children and adolescents with ADD. It is not necessary to embrace one theory over another. Although each theory presents a different view of child development, each offers a useful perspective on how children and adolescents with ADD may be different from their same-age peers. The chapter concludes with a listing of behaviors characteristic of children with ADD at the preschool, elementary, and middle/high school levels.

SOCIAL LEARNING THEORY

Social learning theory emphasizes the role of learning principles such as reinforcement, extinction, punishment, shaping, and imitation in social development. In the context of this theory, children seek acceptance in and security from the social world around them—their parents, teachers, siblings, peers, and community. Their task is to develop behaviors that will empower them to negotiate new relationships and to continue receiving the rewards of existing relationships. In the end, children fit in with the world around them because they have successfully acquired adaptive behaviors via social learning principles.

The following social learning principles apply to all children, whether or not they have ADD: *Reinforcement* refers to anything that strengthens a behavior. For example, if a child receives praise from a classroom teacher for completing independent seatwork and as a result completes independent seatwork more frequently, then teacher praise would be considered a reinforcer. *Extinction* refers to the process whereby a behavior is weakened if reinforcement is removed. For example, if a child's calling out during class discussions has been reinforced by teacher attention, then the removal of teacher attention during calling out will result in the eventual reduction or elimination of this behavior. *Punishment* as a consequence weakens a specific behavior. If writing a letter of apology for hitting another student has the effect of reducing the frequency of hitting episodes, then letter writing would be considered a punishment. *Shaping* refers to the process whereby the child is reinforced for successive approximations toward an ultimate goal. A teacher who praises a student for completing one problem independently at his seat, then praises only after gradually larger amounts of work have been completed, would be using this technique. *Imitation* refers to the process whereby children learn social behavior by observing the behavior of others. For instance, a child may learn to use curse words by observing parents, other children, or even television characters. For more detailed information about social learning theory, see Bandura (1977, 1987).

One particular area in which the child with ADD may experience problems is *observational learning*. The process of observational learning involves four basic components: First, as an attentive observer, the child recognizes the complexities and subtleties of both verbal and nonverbal social exchanges. Second, the child has the capacity to remember whatever is observed. Third, the child is able to reproduce both the language and behavior observed and stored in memory. Finally, upon the child's response, the social environment provides reinforcement, thereby motivating the child to perform similarly in future situations. To illustrate, a child who observes classmates rewarded for completing independent seatwork by being allowed to help with classroom chores (e.g., cleaning the chalkboard) may produce the same response if all the conditions are met: The child has attended to the behavior, remembered the sequence, is able to perform the response, and desires the consequence.

Inattention severely limits the effectiveness of observational learning for the child with ADD. The child with ADD is like someone invited to dinner at a stranger's house in a foreign land. When confronted with a lavish buffet, the dinner guest must inhibit response to internal hunger cues and instead give careful notice to the nuances of this totally unfamiliar social context. In an effort to please and perhaps be invited back, the guest must pay attention to the behaviors that seem appropriate and imitate them in order to make the evening a success. In many situations, the child with ADD has great difficulty inhibiting his or her impulsive response and may fail to attend to the subtleties of social situations. As a result, the child may be perceived as a social misfit.

Social learning theory is not limited to explaining the learning and performance of overt actions but has been expanded to cover cognitive development as well. The principle of *reciprocal determinism* addresses the complex interplay that exists among actions, thoughts, and feelings. The child who does well on a test and who thinks, "I really deserved this grade" will likely have a feeling of mastery and increased self-esteem. On the other hand, the child who is repeatedly reprimanded for getting out of his seat and who thinks, "I'm a real loser" will likely have feelings of dejection and low self-esteem. The child with ADD may become discouraged as a result of the inability to follow rules, understand instructions, and inhibit responses. This may result in a cycle of negative thinking that perpetuates failure at home and at school.

RULE-GOVERNED BEHAVIOR THEORY

A subset of social learning theory, rule-governed behavior theory conceptualizes cognitive and social development in terms of the rules that govern behavior (Barkley, 1981, 1988; Tant & Douglas, 1982). To understand the concept of rule-governed behavior, one must first understand the concept of contingent-governed behavior (i.e., the notion that behavior is learned and maintained through the direct experience of consequences, both positive and negative; Skinner, 1953, 1967). For example, a young child who touches a hot stove and as a consequence experiences pain will learn to avoid touching the stove again. The number of experiences needed to learn this link between action and consequence will vary greatly from child to child according to many factors. These include the ability to attend to relevant cues (e.g., the warmth of the stove), the ability to inhibit certain motor responses (e.g., going into the kitchen), and the ability to regulate activity level (e.g., running carelessly by the hot stove). Other factors such as native intelligence and memory also play a role.

If our survival were solely dependent upon directly experiencing each consequence, our species would become extinct. Fortunately, language communicates information about behavior-consequence connections. Inasmuch as a child's behavior is regulated by a rule (e.g., "Don't touch the hot stove") we would say the child is demonstrating rule-governed behavior. The classroom teacher states a rule (e.g., "Do your work, then you can play a game on the computer") and expects compliance. The majority of the children do comply. These children recognize that their immediate desire to play a game on the computer cannot be indulged until they have performed the other task. Their need for immediate gratification is checked by the standards of conduct imposed by others. Adherence to the rule is reinforced experientially, whereas nonadherence is not reinforced or is actually punished.

Normally, children learn to use rules in a self-regulating fashion, as evidenced by their stating the rule aloud, in their own voice, while their behavior follows suit. In brief, there is a correspondence between what they say and what they do. The preschooler may actually be overheard to say, "I need to hang my coat on the hook" while performing that specific action. As the child engages in repetitions of this "say-do" sequence, the overt verbalization goes "underground," becoming covert as the response becomes automatic. The rules are now internalized and may be consulted in order to determine how to act with different people (e.g., a substitute versus the regular teacher) in different circumstances (e.g., the cafeteria versus the classroom). The child's cognitive and social development is measured by the degree to which he or she conforms to the rules learned.

Given this theoretical framework, the child with ADD can be expected to have significant problems in a wide variety of settings and conditions. The core characteristics of inattention, impulsivity, and hyperactivity make it difficult to pay attention to verbal rules, inhibit response until the rule is followed, and even perform the necessary action in a skilled fashion. Without an internalized set of rules, self-gratification becomes the sole purpose for behavior. The reactions of other people, which usually serve to reinforce rule adherence and guide future behavior, have less impact on the child with ADD because he or she has not processed information that distinguishes appropriate from inappropriate behavior. If reprimanded for not doing assigned classwork, the child with ADD does not reflect on the desired behavior. Rather, the reprimand is seen as blocking the child's wants and needs; as a consequence, the child's frustration increases.

COGNITIVE-DEVELOPMENTAL THEORY

Jean Piaget's cognitive-developmental theory (as discussed in Gins-berg & Opper, 1969) views child development as a reflection of changes in structures of thought. Children adapt to new situations by reorganizing the knowledge they have acquired in past experiences. They struggle to make sense of the world around them by building concepts (i.e., schemas) about new experiences. The two mechanisms used to adjust schemas and adapt to new experiences are assimilation and accommodation.

Assimilation is the process by which a child makes sense of a new experience by referencing past experiences or thought structures. For example, if a third-grade class is told that Ms. Jones will be the substitute teacher in their class that day, and Ms. Jones enters the class and begins teaching a lesson, they will assimilate her into the role of "my teacher." For the child with ADD, the schema or label "my teacher" brings to mind Mr. Smith, the regular teacher, who provides structure and consistency. When Ms. Jones walks into the class, the child with ADD may be confused and may fail to accept the substitute as the authority figure, reacting by testing the limits. In other words, problems develop due to a failure to assimilate the new experience.

Accommodation is the process by which a child recasts the existing definition or schema of a previous experience. In this case, the schema must change to accommodate the new experience of a different person's being the teacher. As the child learns through the new experience that teachers can be temporary as well as permanent, the schema is modified or accommodated. The child with ADD may have difficulty altering his or her view of the teacher role, or take much longer to alter it, thereby being less able to meet the demands of the new situation.

As might be expected, these forms of adaptation apply not only to the learning of labels (i.e., "my teacher") but also to the learning of appropriate behavior. According to cognitive-developmental theory, three factors are at work within each age group: egocentrism, semantics of language, and rule-following skills. Egocentrism is defined as the inability to perceive objects, thoughts, and feelings from another's point of view. As children develop, egocentrism diminishes and perspective taking increases, resulting in the child's increasing ability to display sensitivity and empathy. The second factor, semantics of language, refers to the way in which the salient meanings of words alter behavior. Children gradually learn the various meanings of

words first through contextual cues and later through abstract reasoning. Finally, rule-following skills involve the ability to understand
that rules serve a purpose in governing behavior. Rules gradually
shift in the child's perception from being flexible (designed to suit
the child's purpose), to being fixed, and finally to being fixed but
subject to exception.

Piaget characterized preoperational children, ages 2 through 6,
as inattentive, impulsive, and highly active. Underlying much of this
behavior is a high degree of egocentrism. That is, the child does not
understand that other people may have feelings and beliefs that dif-
fer from his or her own. Everybody has the same perspective—the
child's perspective. In terms of language development, the preoperational child is restricted by the literal meaning of words and expressions. For example, if a classroom teacher tells the child not to bother
handing in classwork if it is not complete, the child may think not
completing the work is actually a viable choice. This absence of reflection or critical thought can also be seen in the area of rule following. A preoperational child sees rules not as rigid, objective standards
to which everyone must conform, but as alterable at will. For example, while playing a game of checkers, the child may decide to
change the rules and move a piece two spaces to avoid losing. Pro-
tests ring hollow because, for the child, rules are just another muta-
ble tool for self-gratification.

As a child moves from the preoperational stage to the stage of
concrete operations, at ages 7 through 11, these behaviors change.
Now a child begins to follow specific rules and routines, readily
adapting to classroom structure. Although the child may recognize
that other people have different thoughts or beliefs, he or she is
likely to ignore or misrepresent these if they threaten the satisfaction
of personal wants and needs. Consequently, the child is rigid and
restricted. This concreteness (i.e., the absence of abstract reasoning)
is also seen in the language and rule-following domains. Although
the child can understand the nuances of words and expressions, he
or she is still most comfortable with literal meanings. The child recognizes objective rules and follows them unquestioningly, unable to
think critically about their purpose or effectiveness.

The adolescent at the stage of early formal operations, at ages
12 through 15, manifests egocentrism in erroneous assumptions regarding other people's thoughts and feelings. A typical case would
involve a teacher's punishing a student for answering out of turn by
sending the student out of the room: The teacher believes doing this
will help the student learn to raise a hand to be recognized. However,
the student believes that the teacher's motives are simply to hurt,
frustrate, or embarrass. Now understanding the subtleties of lan-

guage and the nuances of discrete communications, the student may also invent meaning and coded messages to verify assumptions about a conversation. When asked to meet with a teacher privately, the student's assumption that teachers are threatening may lead him or her to anticipate being chastised. In terms of rule following, the adolescent has begun to think critically about rules and is aware of the consequences of not following them. However, on occasion he or she will decide not to follow the rules, perhaps as an act of defiance or as a means of testing the responses to inappropriate behavior.

This theory of cognitive development sheds light on the problems of the child or adolescent with ADD. Egocentrism, which normally abates with time, instead continues to present a significant handicap to the child's social problem solving. Difficulty in delaying gratification affects the child's ability to engage in long-term planning and to follow rules that may be contrary to the attainment of immediate desires. In terms of adaptation, the child's thought structures are not as neatly organized as those of his or her peers: The processes of assimilation and accommodation are interrupted because the child is not deliberate or reflective enough to manage new information and observations.

COGNITIVE AND SOCIAL LEARNING AT DIFFERENT AGES

Each of the three theories described in this chapter—social learning, rule-governed behavior, and cognitive-developmental—stresses how children's skills vary from one developmental level to another. In making assessments and designing treatments, teachers must consider a child's cognitive and developmental level, tailoring any interventions to the child's expected functional age.

The behaviors in these lists characterize children with ADD in terms of cognitive and social learning at the preschool, elementary, and middle/high school levels, thus illustrating how the developmental functioning of students with ADD differs from that of other students. At the preschool age, unless inattention, impulsivity, and activity are especially problematic, children with ADD are difficult to distinguish. Thus, the list for preschoolers includes behaviors the teacher can expect to see in a majority of students this age. As children who do not have ADD develop, they generally outgrow these behaviors. However, children with ADD continue to experience a number of cognitive and social problems. At the elementary and middle/high school levels, the behavior of students with ADD deviates significantly from that of their peers.

:hool Child

Has difficulty with persistence of effort

Has difficulty delaying self-gratification

Exhibits a high rate of activity

Has difficulty comprehending rules

Has difficulty following rules

Exhibits problems attending to salient cues

Has difficulty with retention

Possesses a narrow behavioral repertoire

Has problems initiating new relationships

Interprets words and expressions literally

Uses language for self-serving purposes

Expects that others will know and meet his or her needs

Has difficulty problem solving

Lacks self-monitoring skills

Elementary School Child

Continues to have difficulty with persistence of effort

Continues to have difficulty delaying gratification

Exhibits a high rate of activity (now labeled "hyperactive")

Believes that rules do not apply if they do not meet his or her own needs

Is unable to sustain attention long enough to glean valuable information

Fails to remember lessons correctly, therefore doing lessons incorrectly or not at all

Has difficulty adjusting to new situations requiring flexibility

Has difficulty with perspective taking

Is insensitive to feedback from others

Depends on the literal meanings of words

Needs brief explanations

Depends on physical rather than verbal communication

Requires adults to provide structure

Breaks problems into steps but looks for immediate solutions

Has difficulty self-monitoring

Middle/High School Adolescent

Still has problems persisting with uninteresting tasks

Delays gratification somewhat but perceives own thoughts and feelings as being more important than those of others

Has a higher activity rate than others

Understands the consequences of inappropriate behavior and learns to live with those consequences

Exhibits improved observation skills but still has difficulty attending to salient cues

Questions utility of subject matter and develops reasons material does not apply to him or her

If interested in subject matter, shows an increased ability to comply with tasks

Strives for responses, positive or negative, from others

Evaluates others' thoughts and feelings in terms of how they affect him or her

Understands language but adjusts the meanings of words and expressions to suit personal needs

Is conversationally functional

Depends on external reinforcement, usually from peers

Knows problem-solving steps but does not follow them

Sees self-monitoring as a behavioral option but is reluctant to change

References

Bandura, A. (1977). *Social learning theory.* New York: Prentice Hall.

Bandura, A. (1987). *Social foundations of thoughts and actions.* New York: Prentice Hall.

Barkley, R. A. (1981). *Hyperactive children: A handbook for diagnosis and treatment.* New York: Guilford.

Barkley, R. A. (1988). Attention Deficit Disorder with Hyperactivity. In E. J. Mash & L. G. Terdal (Eds.), *Behavioral assessment of childhood disorders* (2nd ed., pp. 69–104). New York: Guilford.

Ginsburg, H., & Opper, S. (1969). *Piaget's theory of intellectual development.* Englewood Cliffs, NJ: Prentice Hall.

Skinner, B. F. (1953). *Science and human behavior.* New York: Macmillan.

Skinner, B. F. (1967). *Cumulative record: A selection of papers.* New York: Appleton-Century-Crofts.

Tant, J. L., & Douglas, V. T. (1982). Problem-solving in hyperactive, normal, and reading-disabled boys. *Journal of Abnormal Child Psychology, 10,* 285–306.

4   The Five-Stage Model of Behavioral Assessment

As illustrated by the case examples in chapter 1, significant variability exists among children who share the ADD diagnosis. Whereas some children demonstrate restless, fidgety, and squirmy behavior, others may actually be lethargic. These differences are reflected, in part, by the distinct diagnoses of Attention Deficit Hyperactivity Disorder (ADHD) and Undifferentiated Attention Deficit Disorder (UADD). Children with either of these diagnoses may also be oppositional, defiant, and/or aggressive. Some may be noncompliant due to willful disobedience, whereas others may be noncompliant due to difficulty focusing on the instructions being given. Additional characteristics that show variation are native intelligence, performance on standardized tests, degree of classroom disruption, popularity among peers, gross and fine motor coordination, and self-esteem.

Differences among children with ADD are also evident with regard to responsiveness to various interventions. Although a body of knowledge exists on interventions, we cannot say that what works for one child with ADD will necessarily work for all. For example, although stimulant medication has been a standard of intervention with this population, only 75 to 80% of all children with ADD will respond positively. The remaining 20 to 25% will either not show a positive response to medication or will show a positive response somewhat attenuated by adverse side effects (Barkley, 1977).

Individual differences are not limited to response to medication: They also affect response to behavioral interventions. For example, some children may respond positively to the opportunity to earn rewards (reinforcement), whereas other children may respond better to an intervention where rewards are lost (response cost). Whether a reinforcement program or a response cost intervention will be most effective cannot be decided on an a priori basis. To be most effective, the classroom teacher must carefully assess each child on an individual basis and tailor a classroom behavior change program to meet that individual child's needs. To do so, a methodology is required. The five-stage model of behavioral assessment (Keefe, Kopel, & Gordon, 1978), in use for over 20 years, is described here as a blueprint for designing effective individualized interventions. It includes the following stages: problem identification, measurement and functional analysis, matching intervention to student, assessment of intervention strategies, and evaluation of the intervention plan.

STAGE 1: PROBLEM IDENTIFICATION

The first stage, problem identification, includes a number of tasks: pinpointing presenting problems, determining specific response characteristics, gathering information with regard to history, identifying probable controlling variables, and selecting tentative targets for intervention.

Pinpointing Presenting Problems

Before anything else can be done, it is necessary to determine the exact nature of the child's problem. Sometimes the problems of children with ADD are identified as laziness, stubbornness, lack of motivation, and the like. Traits like these are enduring (permanent) and global (widespread) characteristics demonstrated across time and setting. If we say a child is honest, the information communicated is that the child is honest now and will be honest tomorrow, next week, next month, and next year. In addition, the label implies that the child's honesty does not vary from situation to situation or from person to person.

What happens when negative traits, often used to describe children with attention deficits, are invoked? First, there will be a natural tendency to look for the behavioral referent of the negative trait and to use its occurrence as confirmation of the trait's existence, thereby creating a self-perpetuating system. For example, a child's looking out a window instead of doing seatwork may be seen as evidence of the enduring trait of distractibility. Second, the child's positive actions may be either overlooked or seen as exceptions to the rule. Third, the assumption that the negative trait is permanent and widespread may contribute to a feeling of pessimism. This feeling of pessimism may in turn lead to the conclusion that the child is hopeless or change is impossible, thus creating an atmosphere of passivity and acceptance.

In contrast to trait theory, the behavioral approach emphasizes observable, measurable behavior. Any global characteristic requires an *operational definition* so that the occurrence of the behavior can be agreed upon by two or more observers. Laziness, for example, might be defined as "failure to complete seatwork in math between the hours of 8:30 and 9:15 A.M." Insensitivity to others' feelings might be operationalized as "calling out answers to questions during social studies without first being recognized by the teacher."

Determining Response Characteristics

Once the presenting problems in the classroom have been pinpointed, they should be described in terms of frequency, duration, and/or intensity. Several examples illustrate this process: Ms. J., a fourth-grade teacher, was specifically concerned about children who kept getting out of their seats without permission. She estimated that, of the two children with ADD in her class, one got out of his seat without permission 15 times a day, whereas the other got out of his seat approximately half as many times. Frequency estimates may be highly accurate or inaccurate; nevertheless, they create a starting point for more formal assessments.

Some ADD problems lend themselves to frequency estimates; others are more suited to assessments of duration. These problems include the following, among others: completing independent seatwork, getting in line, making transitions from one academic activity to another, and engaging in tantrums. Mr. R., a special education teacher, was concerned about losing valuable teaching time to transitions from one activity to another. Deciding to use a duration measure, he kept track of the total number of minutes it took for his class to perform a typical six to nine transitions per day. Mr. R.'s concerns were confirmed when he found that over a 5-day period his class averaged 56 minutes per day in transitions!

Intensity, the third key dimension of targeted behaviors, may be used to describe behaviors such as aggression, which may vary along a continuum from a bump of the shoulder to a violent attack. Mrs. N., a second-grade teacher, was worried about a student with ADD who was very aggressive. Noting that his aggression took many forms, she developed a rating scale from 1 to 10, with 10 being the most violent (e.g., biting) and 1 being the least violent (e.g., a threatening gesture).

Obtaining a History of the Problem

A history of the child's problem may be readily obtained from several sources. First, a written record for the child often exists, perhaps even including documentation of interventions carried out by other teachers. A review of the child's records may also provide the results of psychological testing, which may or may not include an evaluation for learning disabilities. In addition, discussions with the child's previous teachers can yield important information about the nature of problems and what approaches have been most effective. Many teachers, concerned about potential bias, are reluctant to use written and/or verbal information from previous teachers. Although the concern is valid, this reluctance often results in "reinventing the wheel" and ultimately contributes to a loss of valuable time. Finally, it is important to acknowledge that parents are a valuable source of historical information and are often eager to collaborate with their child's teacher.

Identifying Probable Controlling Variables

Once presenting problems have been clearly defined and background information gathered, the next step is to identify probable controlling variables. The teacher should make an educated guess as to the circumstances that may set the stage for problem behaviors, as well as the variables that may be involved in maintaining them. In the previous example, Mrs. N. made an educated guess that her student displayed aggressive behavior because he wanted to make friends but lacked the appropriate social skills to do so.

Selecting Tentative Targets for Modification

The end result of this initial stage of behavioral assessment is the selection of tentative targets for intervention. Several guidelines are useful in this regard: First, teachers should select a problem that occurs frequently because this allows for a greater period of study in a shorter period of time. Second, the problem selected should be directly observable. This may mean temporarily bypassing a frequent but unobservable problem occurring in the cafeteria or on the playground in favor of one taking place in the classroom. For problems that occur when the teacher is not present, the assistance of another person will have to be obtained. Finally, a problem should have some educational and/or social significance, for even if a problem occurs at a high frequency and is directly observable it may not be a critical or "keystone" behavior. A child who is highly disruptive, fails to complete seatwork, interrupts, and shows frequent fidgety behavior presents a multitude of possible targets. Although fidgety behavior may be both frequent and observable, the classroom teacher would be wise to choose a target behavior that will make more of a difference to the child's classroom success.

STAGE 2: MEASUREMENT AND FUNCTIONAL ANALYSIS

The main purposes of the measurement and functional analysis stage are to fine-tune the anecdotal information that has been collected and to provide a *baseline* measurement of the child's problem behaviors, or an indication of the preexisting level of behavior. Doing so allows for a conceptualization of the function of the given problem so that an effective personalized intervention can be developed.

Basically, teachers may use two strategies to better understand the child's problem areas: static analysis and functional analysis. A *static analysis* involves the teacher's observing and measuring the target behavior exclusively with reference to frequency, duration, and/or intensity. A *functional analysis* is accomplished by observing the targeted behavior, its antecedents (i.e., that which comes before the target behavior), and its consequences (i.e., that which comes immediately after the target behavior). Antecedents may include specific physical conditions (e.g., seating arrangement), environmental events (e.g., free time), or the behaviors of other children (e.g., name-calling). Knowing that a child's off-task behavior is primarily precipitated by a certain subject matter or time of day can be useful in developing a personalized intervention plan. Consequences are those events or situational factors following the problematic behavior and bearing some relationship to it. A child who has temper tantrums may escape task demands, get increased attention, or obtain a tangible reward such as a preferred seat in the lunchroom. Such consequences may be keys to understanding how to intervene most effectively.

Measurement of Behavior

Additional effort will be required in order to bring about any change in the targeted symptoms of ADD. Classroom teachers, feeling overwhelmed by the amount of effort they must already devote to dealing with off-task or disruptive behavior, may be reluctant to take on additional responsibility for measuring behavior. However, an intervention undertaken without the benefit of formal data collection is unlikely to succeed for a number of reasons.

First, our memories are highly suspect. Imagine that a teacher is working with a youngster who has tremendous difficulty staying seated. The teacher is aware that the child is getting out of his seat constantly and that she is putting forth a great deal of energy redirecting him. The teacher doesn't know exactly how many times the child gets out of his seat during the day—only that it is often. Actually, the child is getting out of his seat at the rate of once every 15 minutes, or 4 times an hour, or 16 times over the course of the 4 hours he spends in the classroom. Suppose an intervention decreases out-of-seat behavior to a daily average of 12 times—a 25% reduction. Without an accurate count of the times the child got out of his seat before the intervention, it would be highly unlikely that the teacher would be able to discriminate this slight but significant improvement. The teacher might be inclined to terminate the intervention prematurely. Even if an intervention is dramatically effective in a short period of time—the child is now getting out of his seat only five times a day—it is possible that the teacher may fail to discriminate this improvement due to other factors, such as the distraction of another child's problematic behavior or stress over applying a new curriculum.

Second, the collection of formal data makes it possible to compare a target child's behavior and the behavior of other children the same age and gender. This kind of comparison allows an appraisal of the severity of difficulties and can help direct limited resources within the school toward the greatest need.

Finally, formal inquiry sets the stage for periodic comparisons— daily, weekly, monthly, or at the beginning and end of the school year—so objective assessment is possible. In brief, this early investment of time and effort pays handsome dividends in the future.

Questionnaires and Other Measures

A variety of specialized questionnaires, checklists, and rating scales have been designed to aid in the assessment of children with ADD. These paper-and-pencil forms provide an assessment of severity, information about any potentially overlooked areas of difficulty, and a baseline from which improvement can be evaluated. Some of the instruments useful to classroom teachers are the Conners' Teacher Rating Scales (CTRS-28; Conners, 1989; Goyette, Conners, & Ulrich, 1978), the ADHD Rating Scale (ADHD-RS; Barkley, 1991), the School Situations Questionnaire (SSQ; Barkley, 1991), and the Academic Performance Rating Scale (APRS; Barkley, 1991).

Observations

Probably the most useful measurements are those that rely on direct observations. Naturalistic observations by the classroom teacher, teacher's assistant, principal, school psychologist, or perhaps even the child provide the baseline from which effective decisions about intervention can be made. When conducted periodically, they also provide information about an intervention's ongoing effects.

Data can be collected by keeping score on a 3 × 5 card, employing a golf wrist-counter, or even using symbolic markers. For example, one fourth-grade teacher was having difficulties with an impulsive student who rarely raised her hand prior to speaking. This teacher was interested in measuring the frequency of calling-out behavior. He used pennies placed in his left pocket as symbolic markers, simply transferring a penny to his right pocket each time the target behavior occurred. At the end of the day he counted the number of pennies in his right pocket, entering this number on the Student Observation Scorecard for Frequency shown in Figure 4.1. (A blank version of this scorecard appears in the Appendix.)

This same teacher initially appraised another child as "never doing his assigned work, always getting out of his seat to sharpen his pencils, and constantly disturbing others." Before designing an intervention to increase on-task behavior, the teacher wanted to measure the duration of the student's current on-task behavior. To do this, he observed the student's behavior during a 30-minute period. Whenever he observed the student working, he started a stopwatch. Whenever the student got out of his seat, talked to neighbors, or worked on unassigned materials, the teacher would stop the watch. When the student returned to work, either on his own or with teacher di-

Figure 4.1   Student Observation Scorecard for Frequency

Student _____*Rhonda*_____ Observer _____*Mr. L.*_____

Target behavior ___*Calling out*_____

Week of ___*10/4/93*___ Time of observation _____*All day*_____

Day	Target behavior (number of times)
Monday	4
Tuesday	9
Wednesday	1
Thursday	3
Friday	8
Total times this week	25
Average per day	5

rection, the teacher would start the watch again. At the end of the 30 minutes, the teacher recorded the time elapsed on the watch (i.e., the total time the child spent working) on the Student Observation Scorecard for Duration illustrated in Figure 4.2. (A blank version of this scorecard appears in the Appendix.)

Another measurement procedure especially useful for classroom teachers is *time sampling*. Time sampling is used to record ongoing behavior, such as paying attention. A teacher who was particularly concerned about whether or not a student was paying attention during group discussions decided to use this method of measurement. She began by dividing the 20 minutes set aside for group discussion into 20 intervals, each a minute long. At the end of each minute, she noted whether the child seemed to be paying attention or not with a plus or a minus on the Student Observation Scorecard for Time Sampling shown in Figure 4.3. (A blank version of this scorecard appears in the Appendix.) At the end of each day's group discussion, the teacher divided the total number of intervals in which the child was observed to be paying attention by the total number of intervals observed. The teacher found that, over a 5-day period, the child had "good days" (80% paying attention) as well as "not-so-good days" (5%

Figure 4.2   Student Observation Scorecard for Duration

Student _____ *Jeff* _____ Observer _____ *Mr. L.* _____

Target behavior _____ *Minutes on task* _____

Week of __ *10/18/93* __ Time of observation __ *10–10:30 A.M. (math)* __

Day	Target behavior (number of minutes)
Monday	14
Tuesday	18
Wednesday	24
Thursday	7
Friday	17
Total minutes this week	80
Average per day	16

paying attention), with an average of 24%. Formal assessment showed that the situation was actually worse than the teacher had originally thought. In addition, it provided a baseline from which to evaluate the effects of future interventions.

Finally, using *self-monitoring*, the child can be enlisted to observe his or her own behavior. Not only does this lighten the teacher's burden, it also develops the student's self-awareness. Self-monitoring proceeds through several phases: teacher monitoring, joint monitoring with the student, and, finally, monitoring by the student alone. Many children underestimate their negative behavior and overestimate their positive behavior without the teacher's external monitoring. In time, this external monitoring can be gradually faded, with a high degree of accuracy being maintained with the teacher's random checking.

Functional Analysis

A functional analysis of a child's presenting problem involves a search for lawful relationships between the target behavior and aspects of the child's environment.

Figure 4.3   Student Observation Scorecard for Time Sampling

Student _____ *Scott* _____ Observer _____ *Mrs. F.* _____

Target behavior _*Paying attention*_____

Week of _*11/8/93*_ Time of observation _____ *9–9:20 A.M.* _____

Period of time sampled _____ *1-minute intervals/20 minutes* _____

Day	Target behavior (+/−)	Daily percentage
Monday		15 %
Tuesday		5 %
Wednesday		80 %
Thursday		10 %
Friday		10 %

Weekly average _____ 24 _____ %

Although developed for use with people with severe developmental disabilities, the Motivation Assessment Scale (MAS; Durand, 1990) can be helpful in conducting functional analyses with children diagnosed with ADD. This 16-item questionnaire assesses rater perceptions of a child's motivations for a specific maladaptive behavior. It is based on the speculation that a given target behavior may have one or more functions: to achieve sensory pleasure, to escape from something unpleasant, to gain attention, and/or to obtain a tangible reward.

For example, Debbie, a second grader diagnosed with ADD, had tremendous difficulty during independent seatwork, as evidenced by her constantly sharpening her pencil, asking to go to the bathroom, and/or wandering around the room looking at the fish tank. Numerous reprimands seemed to have little effect on her behavior, with unfinished classwork the end result. When completed by her teacher, the MAS indicated that the primary motivation for Debbie's getting out of her seat was sensory. In other words, the behavior satisfied her need for physical movement. In order of decreasing importance, it also helped her escape an unpleasant task, obtained the teacher's attention (in the form of reprimands), and netted her tangible rewards. The MAS for Debbie led to an intervention that allowed her the opportunity for more movement in the classroom, modified the difficulty of academic work so she was more likely to succeed, and delivered more teacher attention for positive behavior. Using the MAS to conduct a functional analysis thus helped the teacher personalize Debbie's treatment plan.

Another approach used by classroom teachers to identify probable controlling variables involves the use of an *ABC analysis* (sometimes called a three-term contingency analysis), where A refers to antecedent events (i.e., events that precipitate the target behavior), B refers to the behavior in question, and C refers to the consequences (i.e., what occurs immediately after the target behavior). Anecdotal records can provide the classroom teacher with a rich source of information from which to develop theories about a child's behavior. The case of Billy, age 8, illustrates this approach. Billy engaged in the dangerous behavior of rocking back on his chair, often actually tipping the chair over. The classroom teacher, concerned for Billy's safety, estimated that this behavior occurred 8 to 10 times in a given day. After deciding to perform an ABC analysis, the teacher devised a form consisting of three columns (see Figure 4.4). The first column contained a clear description of the subject matter, lesson being discussed, and so forth (antecedents). The second column contained a detailed description of Billy's actions (behavior). The third column contained the social consequences that occurred. (A blank version of this analysis form appears in the Appendix.)

The information collected led the teacher to conclude that Billy's chair tipping was most probable during independent seatwork; five of the six episodes occurred during this activity. The teacher hypothesized that chair tipping not only allowed Billy to escape seatwork, it also resulted in a tremendous amount of peer attention. This analysis led to a reexamination of the difficulty level of Billy's assigned seatwork, as well as to an instruction to the class not to respond when this behavior occurred. The intervention produced a steady decline in Billy's chair-tipping behavior. Because this method of data collection is very labor intensive, a teacher may choose to use it only for select periods of time (e.g., 30 minutes in the morning and 30 minutes in the afternoon).

Figure 4.4 ABC Analysis for Billy's Chair Tipping

| Student | Billy | Observer | Ms. G. | Date | 12/1/93 |

Antecedents

1. 9:00 A.M.
   (independent math)

2. 10:15 A.M.
   (independent language arts)

3. 11:15 A.M.
   (independent dictionary work)

4. 1:15 P.M.
   (independent science project)

5. 1:45 P.M.
   (group discussion during music)

6. 2:15 P.M.
   (independent reading)

Behavior

1. Chair fell over.

2. Chair fell over; Billy knocked over the desk behind him.

3. Chair fell over; Billy began laughing.

4. Chair fell over; Billy rolled on the floor into another desk.

5. Chair tipped over; Billy hit his head and began crying.

6. Chair tipped over; Billy let out a yell.

Consequences

1. I approached Billy, reprimanded him, and told him to get back into his seat.

2. I reprimanded Billy and told him that he obviously wasn't ready to work and sent him to the back of the room until he was ready to join the class.

3. I ignored Billy and watched him get his chair back up. He began playing with his matchbook cars under his desk.

4. I approached Billy to see if he was hurt. I reprimanded him again and sent him to the principal's office.

5. I ignored Billy and admonished the class for laughing at him, then directed him to get back to his seat.

6. I reprimanded Billy, told him to put his materials away, get his coat, and wait in the principal's office. I instructed him to leave school at dismissal from the office rather than coming back to class.

60

STAGE 3: MATCHING INTERVENTION TO STUDENT

At this stage, all the information gathered is integrated to develop an intervention plan. The major steps involved at this point are as follows: assessing the student's motivation to participate in the intervention, assessing skills and resources, selecting the intervention procedures, and conducting the sharing conference with the child and the child's parents.

Assessing the Student's Motivation

An important factor in deciding what intervention strategies to use is the student's motivation to be an active participant. Some children with ADD may be highly motivated to gain self-control, willing to monitor their own behavior, and capable of engaging in self-reinforcement. Others may have little self-awareness and/or motivation to participate in the treatment plan. A child who may be at this stage initially may require more external control (i.e., responsibility) on the part of the teacher; however, the goal should be to effect a gradual transition to self-reliance.

Assessing Skills and Resources

The second major consideration in choosing an intervention is determining the availability of resources. First, it is important to consider the child's capabilities with regard to memory, intelligence, and temperament. Second, one must assess one's own resources in terms of energy level and knowledge. Some teachers have a great deal of experience and are able to carry out an intervention plan independently, whereas others find it useful to read articles, attend workshops, and/or consult with a school psychologist, guidance counselor, principal, or master-level teacher. Another factor to consider is the cooperation of the child's family. Many children are fortunate to have parents who will not only collaborate with the classroom teacher and provide important insight into the child's interests but also be able to help reinforce gains made in the classroom. Other children are not so fortunate, and responsibility for change may fall largely on the teacher and others in the school environment.

Selecting Intervention Procedures

Several useful guidelines have emerged for selecting intervention procedures. First, the classroom teacher should choose the intervention on the basis of its simplicity and ease of administration. Second, the literature should to some degree support the intervention's effectiveness for children with ADD. Finally, the plan should meet with administrative and parental approval, especially if the intervention goes beyond what is customary for the classroom, contains aversive elements, or may cause parental concern.

Conducting the Sharing Conference

Before beginning any intervention plan, the classroom teacher and other concerned school personnel should meet with the child and the child's parents. During this sharing conference, the nature of the presenting problem should be outlined and the reasons for intervention delineated. In addition, any specific data that have been collected should be presented. Care should be taken to outline the details of the intervention plan and to link the plan directly to the information gathered. Finally, all concerned should agree on the goals of the intervention.

It is useful to have all information readily available and to follow these steps when conducting the conference:

1. Describe the child's strengths.

2. Describe the child's problems. Be specific.

3. Present findings from specific ADD rating scales.

4. Present data from various student observation scorecards.

5. Specify reason(s) for intervening.

6. Establish an atmosphere of collaboration.

7. Develop the intervention plan.

8. Obtain informed written consent.

9. Establish a system of communication between home and school.

STAGE 4: ASSESSMENT OF INTERVENTION STRATEGIES

A major strength of the five-stage model is that assessment does not stop once the intervention plan is put into effect. Rather, continual evaluation occurs parallel to the application of interventions. Three major tasks exist at this stage: checking the application of the intervention, monitoring the effectiveness of the procedures, and making modifications to the intervention plan when necessary. Stage 4 can be carried out by the teacher alone or in conjunction with the student during regular meetings. The teacher may also wish to consult periodically with another professional knowledgeable about ADD.

Checking the Application of the Intervention

At this stage the teacher needs to ask first whether the plan is being used and second how well the plan is being applied. For example, if a plan involves providing positive feedback for on-task behavior during independent seatwork between 10:00 and 10:30 A.M., then the actual provision of such feedback may need to be verified. An independent observer (e.g., a colleague or the principal) may help check the frequency. Alternatively, the teacher may engage in self-monitoring by noting each occurrence of positive feedback on a private scorecard. This proverbial "string around the finger" cues the teacher to use the plan.

A more subtle assessment is required to determine how well the plan is being applied. For example, positive feedback can be given in a bland monotone, or it can be given enthusiastically. Thus, there may be significant qualitative differences in the way the positive feedback is delivered. If audiotape or videotape equipment is available, it can be a powerful tool for fine-tuning one's application of an intervention plan.

Monitoring the Effectiveness of Procedures

Once it has been determined that the procedures are, in fact, being appropriately applied, it is time to address the issue of whether or not the stated goals are being met. Is medication having the desired effect? What are the results of a new seating arrangement? Has assigning a playground companion actually decreased negative incidents at recess? Is a point system increasing the amount of classwork completed? The responsive teacher does not wait months before attempting to answer these and other questions. Data should be collected on an ongoing basis—hourly, daily, weekly, and/or monthly, depending upon the target behavior and the available resources. The methods outlined in Stage 2 for measurement and functional analysis can be helpful in monitoring change.

Modifying the Intervention Plan

If the collected data reveal insufficient change, the teacher must consider whether the intervention needs to be altered or whether the overall conceptualization of the problem needs to be reevaluated. Interventions require constant attention, for although desired results may be obtained for a period of time it is quite common for such results to be short lived. Regression to previous levels of behavior is common as the novelty of an intervention wears off. Thus, it is wise to anticipate regression by building in novelty (e.g., injecting new rewards every week or so).

In addition, the problem may need to be reconceptualized, with the result being a different approach altogether. For example, John, age 6, was in a transitional kindergarten due to severe ADD. During arts and crafts tasks, he often became silly and broke many classroom rules. After implementing Stages 1, 2, and 3 of the five-stage model, the teacher began a time-out procedure—brief isolation immediately after John's inappropriate behavior. Unfortunately, there was little reduction in John's acting out. Closer examination revealed that John's behavior was motivated not by his need to gain attention but rather by his need to escape from arts and crafts, an activity he found unpleasant. Thus, the time-out was actually maintaining the problem. An intervention designed to make the task more attractive by providing several choices turned out to be quite effective.

STAGE 5: EVALUATION OF THE INTERVENTION PLAN

The classroom teacher who has followed the procedures just described is in an excellent position to evaluate whether or not desired objectives have been achieved. Measurements taken prior to the development of a classroom behavior change project and during the course of the intervention provide the basis for evaluating change.

One important factor is the degree to which participants are satisfied not only with the end results but also with the methods used to obtain these results. This is referred to as *social validation*. Satisfaction with the outcome and methods can be assessed among child, parents, teachers, peers, and administrators. Although there will be little satisfaction if the end results are not as desired, what may be less obvious is that achieving a desired outcome with methods viewed as distasteful (e.g., withholding certain privileges, using time-out) will most likely result in a drift away from the use of these procedures over time. In brief, without social validation, gains are unlikely to be maintained.

Because ADD is a chronic condition—likely to persist over time and across settings—the question of maintaining gains is especially important. Special procedures may be cumbersome and unnatural in the sense that other children do not require their use. However, these accommodations may be necessary for long-term success. Periodic assessments are warranted to determine whether improvements can be maintained with less intrusive methods, but interventions may need to be reinstated or modified as the demands of the situation change. Consistency is a key component in addressing the needs of children with ADD.

References

Barkley, R. A. (1977). A review of stimulant drug research with hyperactive children. *Journal of Child Psychology and Psychiatry, 5*, 351–369.

Barkley, R. A. (1991). *Attention Deficit Hyperactivity Disorder: A clinical workbook.* New York: Guilford.

Conners, C. K. (1989). *Conners' Teacher Rating Scales manual.* North Tonawanda, NY: Multi-Health Systems.

Durand, V. M. (1990). *Severe behavior problems: A functional communication training approach.* New York: Guilford.

Goyette, C. H., Conners, C. K., & Ulrich, R. F. (1978). Normative data on revised Conners' Parent and Teacher Rating Scales. *Journal of Abnormal Child Psychology, 6*, 221–236.

Keefe, F. J., Kopel, S. A., & Gordon, S. B. (1978). *A practical guide to behavioral assessment.* New York: Springer.

5 Methods of Gathering Data

The major methods used in the five-stage model of behavioral assessment (Keefe, Kopel, & Gordon, 1978) are structured interviews and questionnaires, behavior rating scales and checklists, naturalistic observations, and objective tests. These methods are used to gather data to help form a comprehensive picture of the child with ADD. Using them within the context of the five-stage model lays the foundation for successful intervention. This chapter uses the case examples from chapter 1 to illustrate how these various assessment methods can be applied for the purposes of diagnosis, development of classroom interventions, and, finally, evaluation.

STRUCTURED INTERVIEWS AND QUESTIONNAIRES

In all likelihood, teachers will participate in a structured interview to convey information to parents, the school principal, other school personnel, and/or psychologists with whom the family may have consulted. In one such structured interview, George's third-grade teacher, Ms. A., was asked to describe George's behavior.

> Dr. G.: Could you please tell me which of George's actions you would like to see occur less often? The more specific you can be the better.
>
> Ms. A.: Well, George can't stay in his seat, and he can't keep his hands to himself.

Dr. G.: That's a good start. So two things you'd like to see George do less of is getting out of his seat and touching other students?

Ms. A.: Yes. If we could accomplish those two things, then George would be able to keep up with the class and wouldn't get in so much trouble. I'd also like to decrease his calling out in class.

Dr. G.: OK, so you've identified three actions or targets you'd like to see occur less often. Are there things you'd like to see George do more often or would like to see increased?

Ms. A.: What do you mean?

Dr. G.: Well, it's not enough simply to eliminate inappropriate behavior without strengthening appropriate behavior because we would just run the risk of having George substitute some other problem in its place.

Ms. A.: I see what you mean. He rarely completes his daily work in school, so I guess I'd like to increase the completion of classwork. George also has some serious problems in the lunchroom and on the playground, but I'm not there at those times, so I just hear about it from the teacher in charge or from the other children, who seem to delight in telling me that he got into trouble.

Dr. G.: So in addition to decreasing getting out of his seat, touching others, and calling out, we also want to increase the completion of classwork. As for the problems that occur when you aren't present, I would suggest we hold off on addressing those problems until we can meet with the other teacher.

The structured interview proceeds in this fashion until all the child's problems are specified. It is typical to have a long list of behaviors to decrease and a shorter list of behaviors to increase. Teachers who prepare this list prior to meeting with the child's parents or other school personnel will greatly facilitate the process. Suggested target behaviors to increase and decrease are presented in Table 5.1.

Table 5.1   Target Behaviors to Increase and Decrease

Increase	Decrease
1. Looking at relevant cues	1. Looking around the room
2. Responding correctly	2. Daydreaming
3. Raising hand	3. Calling out
4. Waiting to speak	4. Interrupting
5. Sitting in seat	5. Getting out of seat
6. Remaining in designated area	6. Wandering around the room
7. Following instructions	7. Not following instructions
8. Waiting for instructions	8. Starting tasks before instructions
9. Expressing anger positively	9. Name-calling
10. Initiating conversation	10. Teasing
11. Requesting help	11. Taking property of others
12. Working independently	12. Hitting
13. Completing assignments	13. Touching others
14. Volunteering answers	14. Having angry outbursts
15. Talking quietly	15. Talking loudly
16. Having materials	16. Losing materials
17. _____	17. _____
18. _____	18. _____
19. _____	19. _____
20. _____	20. _____

After all the problems are specified, the interview focuses on estimated frequency of their occurrence, as well as on the circumstances under which they occur. This information provides a preliminary idea of the frequency of the behaviors before intervention (i.e., a baseline) and alerts the teacher and others to the severity of the problems and possible areas for intervention.

> Dr. G.:   You've indicated that one of the most severe problems occurs when George has to do

independent seatwork. Is it all types of work or
only certain subjects?

Ms. A.: It doesn't seem to matter whether it's language
arts or reading, but it doesn't happen as much
during math.

Dr. G.: Let's take a look at those three subjects. Are those
the only subjects where he is expected to work
independently at his seat?

Ms. A.: That's it, pretty much.

Dr. G.: I'd like you to estimate as best you can how often
he engages in disturbing behaviors during each of
these subjects.

The interview continues in this fashion until estimated baselines are
established. In addition, hypotheses are developed as to the function
of the particular behavior. By asking questions about how the environment responds to George when he engages in off-task or disturbing behavior, we may begin to understand his motivation better.
Once we understand his motivation, we can develop a classroom intervention to address these problems. George may be getting out of
his seat during independent work to get attention from the teacher
and/or his peers, to obtain something tangible (at times Ms. A. has
instructed George to do his work in the bean-bag chair in a corner of
the room), to escape what he perceives to be a difficult or unpleasant
task, or to satisfy his unique need for extra movement.

The teacher's ratings on one particular questionnaire, the Motivation Assessment Scale (MAS; Durand, 1990), described in chapter 4,
helped answer these questions. In George's case it seemed that his
primary motivations were for escape from an unpleasant task followed by the desire for extra movement. Recognizing both escape
from an unpleasant task and the need for movement as legitimate
functions, the teacher and consultant designed an intervention that
included an appropriate means for George to achieve these ends,
thereby eliminating the need for his disturbing behaviors. Specifically, modifications were made in the duration and complexity of
George's independent classwork. George was also instructed to get
up and approach the teacher for corrective feedback as soon as he
had worked for 5 minutes. (He kept track of the time he had worked
by moving the hands of a construction paper clock taped to his desk.)

These two interventions led to a gradual improvement in the completion rate and accuracy of George's classwork, as well as to a reduction in the frequency of his disturbing behaviors.

Structured interviews and questionnaires need to be repeated throughout the various stages of assessment, with particular attention being given to the changes that occur in the child's behavior over time. Whether working with a consultant or meeting the challenge alone, the classroom teacher can benefit greatly by using these methods.

BEHAVIOR RATING SCALES AND CHECKLISTS

Behavior rating scales and checklists have many advantages. Among these are the ability to address problem areas that might unintentionally be overlooked, establish a baseline from which to evaluate the effectiveness of classroom interventions, provide a reference group for comparison, and assess severity of ADD. Behavior rating scales and checklists are also valuable in providing feedback to pediatricians and parents with regard to a child's responsiveness to stimulant medication.

Jacky's teacher completed four assessment measures to help gather information that would lead to a diagnosis: the Conners' Teacher Rating Scale (CTRS-28; Conners, 1989; Goyette, Conners, & Ulrich, 1978), the ADHD Rating Scale (ADHD-RS; Barkley, 1991), the School Situations Questionnaire (SSQ; Barkley, 1991), and the Academic Performance Rating Scale (APRS; Barkley, 1991).

The CTRS-28 has been used as a quick screening assessment for conduct problems, hyperactivity, and inattention-passive behaviors displayed in a classroom setting. It is most useful for providing a general assessment of the child with ADD and for assessing medication and treatment effects. In Jacky's case this measure yielded a profile with elevations on the hyperactivity and inattention indexes.

The ADHD-RS is a list of the 14 behavioral symptoms of ADHD outlined in the *Diagnostic and Statistical Manual of Mental Disorders* (DSM-III-R; American Psychiatric Association, 1987). It can serve as a quick screening of ADHD symptoms as well as provide a severity rating of each. It also assesses, by gender and age, the degree of inattention and impulsivity-hyperactivity in comparison with that of other children. Jacky's teacher endorsed the presence of 9 of the 14 symptoms on the ADHD-RS, giving her an extreme score on the inattention factor (i.e., "Often does not seem to listen").

Developed for both general assessment and evaluation of treatment outcome, the SSQ provides 12 behavioral areas of classroom and school behavior and gives a severity rating for each. The information it taps is useful in identifying targets for intervention and in evaluating treatments. The SSQ for Jacky indicated problems in 5 of the 12 areas (e.g., individual deskwork).

The APRS assesses academic productivity as well as accuracy of classwork and class participation. This measure evaluates four specific areas: learning ability, impulse control, academic performance, and social withdrawal. The APRS indicated that Jacky's greatest difficulty was in completing her work rather than in its accuracy.

The results of these four completed rating scales led to Jacky's diagnosis of Undifferentiated Attention Deficit Disorder, or UADD (by many still referred to as ADD without hyperactivity, or ADD/−H).

Another type of rating scale useful in selected situations is the *peer nomination method*, which provides information about a child's social standing among peers. When the child with ADD is suspected of having peer relationship difficulties, peer nomination can confirm or refute this suspicion. In addition, it can also provide a baseline against which to judge the impact of social skills training or other interventions. Four of Dennis's teachers helped gather this type of information by passing out 3 × 5 cards to each student and asking them to write down, anonymously, the names of three students with whom they would like to study and the names of three students with whom they would like to "hang out." A rank ordering of these two lists revealed a clear pattern: Dennis was in the bottom third for all four classes regardless of the form of the question. These results are shown in Table 5.2.

NATURALISTIC OBSERVATIONS

Naturalistic observations may be the most significant of all the various assessment methods available, for the observer directly studies the problems in question and makes minimal inferences from them. Ms. A., George's third-grade teacher, was particularly interested in observing and measuring the degree to which George was on task during 30 minutes of independent seatwork. After arriving at a careful definition of on-task behavior (i.e., George in his seat, assigned materials on his desk opened to the correct page, pencil in hand, looking at materials and/or writing answers), she decided to use a time-sampling method (see chapter 4). She divided the block of time

**Table 5.2   Social Ranking for Dennis Based on Peer
Nomination Method**

Class	Number of students	Ranking for studying	Ranking for "hanging out"
1	20	20	18
2	21	17	15
3	23	23	19
4	18	18	14

into 10 intervals of 3 minutes each. At the end of each interval, she glanced at George and noted on a scorecard a plus if he was on task and a minus if he was off task. During this baseline assessment, she continued to deal with George in whatever way she felt appropriate. At the end of the period she noted the number of observed intervals of plus behavior and divided that by the total number of observed intervals. Over a 5-day period, George's on-task scores ranged from a low of 10% to a high of 60%, with the average being approximately 25%. This overall assessment revealed that George was actually off task far more often than Ms. A. had originally thought and led to her hypothesis that George's behavior was motivated primarily by his desire for activity and attention. A combined classroom intervention involving medication, teacher attention, and a planned activity schedule brought about significant improvement.

Jacky's teacher, Mr. Q., was primarily concerned about how long it took Jacky to complete classwork and about the fact that so much of her unfinished work was sent home to be completed, often resulting in major battles on the home front, sometimes lasting for up to 5 hours. He decided to establish a data base to address this problem. Because the number of assignments varied from day to day, he decided to collect the data as a percentage of classwork completed. He checked Jacky's work daily and privately compared the number of assignments completed to the total number of assignments given. Over a 2-week period, Jacky's scores ranged from a low of 40% to a high of 100%, with an average of approximately 60%. Most of the other children in the class were closer to 100%. This data base, in combination with information from teacher observations and formal testing, suggested that Jacky's difficulties were due in part to a slower speed of processing information. A classroom intervention using medication, positive incentives, and smaller amounts of work was found to be very effective.

Social behaviors can also be targeted for naturalistic observation, as illustrated in Dennis's case. Dennis's social studies teacher, Mr. L., wanted to address Dennis's calling out in class, whether his calling out was relevant to the discussion or not (e.g., concerning something interesting on television). Mr. L. began by developing a private score-card, on which he tallied each call-out. After 5 days he found that Dennis's call-outs ranged from a low of three to a high of nine, with an average of seven. Mr. L. took the naturalistic observation one step further by meeting privately with Dennis, explaining what he had been doing and asking Dennis if he would be willing to try an experiment. Mr. L. would continue to keep a record of Dennis's call-outs, and Dennis would keep his own record. At the end of the class period they would compare their scores. If there was a match, then Dennis could earn extra time with the computer graphic arts software, something for which he had been asking. This example illustrates that naturalistic observations, typically done by someone other than the child, can with careful consideration include the child's input. Direct engagement in self-observation can thus become the first step in the child's acquisition of self-control.

OBJECTIVE TESTS

Intelligence tests, achievement tests, and aptitude tests of various sorts have long been part of ADD evaluation. Because their benefits and limitations have been capably described elsewhere (see Barkley, 1991), they will not be discussed at length here. Recently, however, we have found one objective test particularly valuable in conducting a comprehensive diagnostic evaluation. The Test of Variables of Attention (T.O.V.A.) is a neuropsychological continuous performance test that requires the test taker to attend to one of two symbols appearing very briefly on a computer screen. The subject must press a switch when one symbol (a square with a hole at the top) appears and not when another (a square with a hole at the bottom) appears. The test is introduced as the "paying attention game," and most children seem to have no difficulty understanding the directions. In addition to formal scores, careful observations of the child's behavior during the test (which in truth is extremely boring) can also help in detecting ADD. Formal scores are developed in four areas and are then used to differentiate children with ADD from the general population. These areas—inattention, impulsivity, response time (a measure of speed of processing information) and variability (a measure of consistency)—are interpreted in the same fashion as IQ scores, with a mean of 100 and a standard deviation of 15. A more detailed account of the development of the T.O.V.A. and its uses can be found in Greenberg (1991).

George, Jacky, and Dennis were each administered the T.O.V.A. as part of an initial evaluation. Because all the available data suggested that they had significant impairment, each was administered a challenge dose of stimulant medication, or a dose designed to determine a child's responsiveness. Approximately 1.5 hours after taking the medication, each was readministered the T.O.V.A. As Table 5.3 illustrates, all of the children responded positively to the challenge dose. This resulted in the incorporation of medication into each child's overall classroom intervention.

Table 5.3   T.O.V.A. Scores for George, Jacky, and Dennis Under Baseline (BL) and Challenge (C) Doses of Stimulant Medication

	George		Jacky		Dennis	
Variable of attention	**BL**	**C**	**BL**	**C**	**BL**	**C**
Inattention	75	102	105	111	94	103
Impulsivity	92	106	101	108	81	88
Response time	61	107	52	81	47	93
Variability	83	98	77	92	72	98

References

American Psychiatric Association. (1987). *Diagnostic and statistical manual of mental disorders* (3rd ed. rev.). Washington, DC: Author.

Barkley, R. A. (1991). *Attention Deficit Hyperactivity Disorder: A clinical workbook.* New York: Guilford.

Conners, C. K. (1989). *Conners' Teacher Rating Scales manual.* North Tonawanda, NY: Multi-Health Systems.

Durand, V. M. (1990). *Severe behavior problems: A functional communication training approach.* New York: Guilford.

Goyette, C. H., Conners, C. K., & Ulrich, R. F. (1978). Normative data on revised Conners' Parent and Teacher Rating Scales. *Journal of Abnormal Child Psychology, 6,* 221–236.

Greenberg, L. M. (1991). *T.O.V.A. interpretation manual: Test of Variables of Attention computer program.* Minneapolis: University of Minnesota.

Keefe, F. J., Kopel, S. A., & Gordon, S. B. (1978). *A practical guide to behavioral assessment.* New York: Springer.

6   Issues Underlying Successful Interventions

In our experience, many intervention strategies look good on paper but fail because certain basic issues have not been directly addressed. This chapter will discuss these issues in the hope that doing so will improve the chances that the specific interventions teachers develop will be successful.

ADD as a Handicapping Condition

ADD is a handicapping condition just like a physical or sensory disability. Educational accommodations are required for the child with ADD just as they would be for the child who uses a wheelchair or a hearing aid. Unfortunately, ADD is still sometimes perceived as a diagnostic fad or a sign of a character defect such as laziness or stubbornness. Before meaningful interventions can be undertaken, the syndrome of ADD must be recognized as "real."

Teachers: Technicians or Professionals?

Much of the behavior management material written for classroom teachers is organized by specific problem (e.g., calling out or failure to complete assignments). This "cookbook approach" offers a number of possible solutions but tends to view teachers as technicians who will apply certain methods without understanding the motivation behind the behavior in question. One such resource identified the problem of the child's rocking in his or her chair, then went on to enumerate suggestions as if to imply that the teacher-technician should start at the top and work down until the problem is solved!

The teacher is much more than a technician. Rather, he or she is a professional able to understand the nature of ADD, analyze the problem carefully, select an appropriate target for intervention, define and measure that target, systematically intervene with an approach logically connected to the function of the target behavior, and evaluate the effectiveness of the intervention. Unless the teacher is involved at this level, the intervention has little chance of success.

Investment of Time and Energy

As consultants, we often hear from teachers the familiar refrain "But I'm already spending too much of my time with this child as it is!" It is an unfortunate truth that, even though teachers are already expending a great deal of effort, they will need to expend more to make interventions work. Some of this additional effort involves becoming knowledgeable about ADD—reading articles, books, and handouts. We also strongly recommend that teachers attend workshops, lectures, and seminars on the topic. Ms. A., George's teacher, was able to attend an inservice workshop on ADD and received some literature from George's parents, which she promptly read. Jacky's teacher, Mr. Q., actually accompanied Jacky's mother to an ADD parent support group to hear a lecture on educational accommodations for children with ADD. Dennis was less fortunate, perhaps in part because as a high school student he interacted with many teachers, each having preconceived ideas about his behavior.

Data collection is another area in which additional effort will be required. A classroom behavior change project cannot be expected to succeed in the absence of a data base. The data base is essential for accountability as well as to ensure that effective intervention plans are maintained and ineffective plans are rapidly modified. In addition, teachers will need to fill out rating scales, questionnaires, and checklists during the initial evaluation phase and on a continuing basis to provide feedback to the child, parents, and any mental health professionals who may be involved (see chapter 5).

Time must also be set aside for formal meetings with the child, parents, other educators, and mental health consultants. These meetings may cut into other teaching or even personal time, but they are necessary for long-term success.

Finally, teachers will need to exercise a great deal of tolerance for behavior that may not be the norm. Because the child's behavior may contribute to anger and frustration, more effort to maintain control over one's own emotions will be required.

The demands of working with the child with ADD may initially seem daunting. However, in the long run the effort expended will result in a better classroom experience for both child and teacher. The time it takes to implement changes will decrease as procedures become more routine. It is also truly heartening to observe real improvements in a student's performance as a result of one's efforts.

Directive Versus Nondirective Teaching Philosophy

Teachers vary in the degree to which they are directive versus nondirective. A nondirective educator values less structured and more spontaneous teaching, whereas a directive teacher values structure and emphasizes planning ahead. Each style has its advantages and disadvantages. Although no scientific data exist to support this contention, our clinical experience suggests that children with ADD do better when the expectations for their behavior are clear and consistent and when their behavior is dealt with contingently (i.e., cause and effect relationships exist between behaviors and consequences). Therefore, the more directive teaching style will more likely create the educational environment that will meet the needs of children with ADD.

Contact With Collateral Individuals

Because children with ADD present challenges both at home and in school, teachers must be prepared to collaborate with parents and other involved professionals, such as psychologists, private tutors, and pediatricians. The benefits of a consistent approach across the entire day for the child with ADD cannot be overemphasized. If the classroom teacher is using an effective approach in school, then the parents may benefit from using it at home. Likewise, parents may have developed a successful home intervention plan that could be adapted for school.

Communication is especially important with regard to the use of stimulant medication. Teachers will need to keep parents, psychologists, and/or pediatricians apprised of the effects of medication if it is part of the overall treatment plan. In many cases the effects of medication are visible only to the classroom teacher.

Attentional Differences in Children With ADD

Children with ADD have attentional differences that help explain their problems with inattention, impulsivity, and hyperactivity. The concepts of the Stimulation Comfort Zone and Attentional Bias to Novelty are central in this regard.

The Stimulation Comfort Zone

Basically, the Stimulation Comfort Zone, or SCZ, is the level of physical and mental activity that provides us with a sense of psychological balance and equilibrium. The level at which someone feels comfortable varies greatly from person to person. A television commercial for a vacation spot may help illustrate: The commercial shows people snorkeling, water skiing, playing tennis, golfing, sailing, doing aerobics, and dancing into the wee hours of the morning. A voice-over narration then states that another option is doing nothing at all. The accompanying visual is of a person relaxing in a lounge chair on the beach with a clear, beautiful sky in the background. As the commercial shows, what constitutes a satisfying vacation is a personal matter. One individual may play beach volleyball and tennis, do aerobics, and sail—all before lunch. Another is happiest lying prone with a good book, rising only for meals. In each case, the person is trying to reach his or her own SCZ.

The SCZ is not static but may vary within an individual at different times. To reach our own personal SCZ, we adjust our covert (mental) and overt (physical) behavior on an ongoing basis. If we experience more stimulation than is comfortable, we attempt to reduce or terminate that stimulation, even if temporarily. For example, participants in a three-way conversation in which everyone is speaking at once may become agitated when trying to process all the input. Someone will probably attempt to slow things down by suggesting that only one person speak at a time. Another person may feel the need to leave a tavern because the music is too loud or the patrons too raucous. We may also seek to increase stimulation when we feel understimulated. At another time, a person may decide to participate in every vacation activity from sunup to sundown or seek out the noisy tavern.

Some adults do of course attempt to find their SCZ by engaging in potentially dangerous or maladaptive behaviors, such as abusing drugs and alcohol or driving recklessly. However, most of us will engage in healthy, adaptive behaviors to modulate our SCZs.

Attentional Bias to Novelty

A concept related to the SCZ is Attentional Bias to Novelty. Central to this idea is the assumption that in children with ADD the area of the brain responsible for attention, concentration, and the ability to inhibit motor responding is in a state of underarousal, not overarousal, as had been previously held.

Dr. Sydney Zentall and her colleagues (Zentall, 1985, 1993; Zentall, Falkenberg, & Smith, 1985) investigated the overarousal theory by placing children with ADD in a classroom setting barren of stimulation. The setting was similar to the classroom environments recommended for these children on the basis of the overarousal theory. Zentall found that children with ADD actually did better under more stimulating conditions. When faced with an environment or activity they perceived dull, the children created their own stimulation, often in a maladaptive manner. Zentall concluded that children with ADD are underaroused in the classroom and that many of their symptoms are simply their attempts to increase stimulation and reach their own personal SCZ. Thus, sensory stimulation on various levels (e.g., Christmas lights strung about the room, teachers' wearing colorful clothing and accessories, children's remaining with their peers rather than being separated) may actually increase, not decrease, concentration in children with ADD.

Zentall's findings may also explain why we often hear laments like "How can he possibly have ADD when he can sit and play Nintendo for hours?" or "She can't have ADD because if it's something that interests her, she can pay attention!" Nintendo or other active, exciting, and novel activities bring children with ADD into their personal SCZ. When the activity is boring to begin with or ceases to be novel, the child with ADD will likely engage in covert (e.g., daydreaming) and/or overt (e.g., repeatedly going to the bathroom) behaviors to increase stimulation.

Implications for educational accommodations

As we begin to look at the characteristics of the child with ADD through the prism of the SCZ and Attentional Bias to Novelty, we can begin to comprehend the motivations that drive the child's maladaptive behaviors, make predictions about what types of tasks are going to be difficult for the child, and, finally, determine the environmental accommodations the classroom teacher needs to make.

Examining the three primary characteristics of ADD (i.e., inattention, impulsivity, and hyperactivity) through this prism makes it clear that the child's failure to pay attention is the result of boredom with the activity. The motivation to engage in maladaptive behavior is to increase the level of stimulation. Thus, the child will seek out aspects of the world that may be more interesting than what the class is doing—even a piece of lint to twirl may provide the needed stimulation. Similarly, impulsive and hyperactive behaviors are motivated by a desire to create stimulation. Impulsivity is often manifested in having difficulty with multiple choice tests (i.e., choosing the first answer), being unable to follow directions (e.g., acting before the full direction is given), and being incapable of the planning and organization required to complete long-term projects. Hyperactivity—characterized by squirminess, restlessness, and fidgetiness—provides increased stimulation through the child's motor system.

Once the teacher understands why the child is unable to remain on task in class and can make an educated guess about which activities will prove difficult for the child, environmental accommodations can be made. For example, it has commonly been assumed that forcing a child to sit still improves learning. However, it may well be that learning is enhanced for the child with ADD when activity and discussion are allowed and encouraged. The classroom teacher can safely predict that *familiar* topics in *familiar* settings involving *repetition* will be problematic for children with ADD. Memorizing lists of names and dates, studying spelling words, and the like will elicit the standard refrain: "Boring!"

ADD's effects on the child's schooling are not limited to the symptoms just described. Numerous associated problems also require attention. For example, children with ADD often perform as well as their peers on new tasks. However, with repetition the tasks lose their novelty, and the child with ADD begins to compensate for boredom through maladaptive behavior. Not only does the failure to finish *routine* (a key word) classroom assignments lead to punishment, it often results in the child's being given the unfinished classwork to do in place of recess. Frequently the incomplete work must be done at home. Parents of children with ADD wonder if it is normal for their child to have so much homework. It becomes necessary to explain that there are two types of homework: regular homework and work the child did not attempt or finish in class. The longer the class assignment, the more difficult it will be for the child to maintain attention. The same problem makes homework completion harder for the child with ADD. To sit at the kitchen table filling out pages in a workbook while friends are playing outside or siblings are watching television may seem like torture.

Another associated problem is failure to adhere to classroom rules (e.g., raising a hand to speak, staying seated, using materials in a proper manner). We find that many children with ADD show greater rule adherence the first 2 months of each school year. This improvement serves to raise the hopes of anxious parents. However, there is a gradual deterioration in the child's performance in the ensuing months. This pattern is often repeated yearly. The novelty of a new physical space, a new teacher, new children, new books, and a new schedule may contribute to the child's increased compliance at the beginning of each school year. As time goes on, the need for novelty resurfaces. If the teacher doesn't stimulate the child's interest, then the child will try to find stimulation elsewhere. In such a case it is more than likely that the child will engage in maladaptive and disruptive behavior.

Another significant problem for children with ADD is difficulty with peer relationships. Their preference for novelty may make it hard to play games by the same rules every day. It may be difficult for them to share because this means waiting while someone else uses what they have found interesting. It is also significant that children with ADD often like loud, sometimes "wild" play as opposed to quiet, slower paced games or activities. They also often engage in provocative behavior that elicits screaming, arguing, and combativeness. A common complaint of teachers and parents alike is "It seems like he *wants* me to yell at him." In a sense this is true: Strong emotional responses, typically negative ones, grab the attention of the child with ADD.

A Positive Approach

Children with ADD, especially those who demonstrate so-called garlic symptoms (see chapter 1), often make it difficult for peers, teachers, and even their own parents to develop positive reciprocal relationships. It is easy to fall into the trap of seeing only these children's weaknesses and remaining blind to their many strengths, but it is necessary to consider their positive qualities when designing interventions.

One child with ADD displayed numerous disturbing behaviors in his after school program, engaging in frequent name-calling, teasing, and general defiance, especially during athletic games. He was quite skilled but had little tolerance for other children who were less so. The teacher involved in the after school program, with whom the child had a positive relationship, reported that she actually liked his enthusiasm in spite of all his difficulties. An experimental plan was developed in which this teacher asked the child to become an assistant coach and practice "good coaching techniques." The latter were described as offering praise after another child's skillful display (e.g., "Good shot!") or encouragement after a less-than-skillful display (e.g., "Nice try. You'll do it next time"). The child approached the task with great enthusiasm; over a matter of several weeks his behavior improved dramatically. Although the results are not so dramatic in every situation, this case does illustrate the importance of recognizing something positive in each child and using that quality to help the child develop increased feelings of self-worth.

References

Zentall, S. S. (1985). A contest for hyperactivity. In K. D. Gadow & I. Bialer (Eds.), *Advances in learning and behavioral disabilities* (Vol. 4, pp. 273–343). Greenwich, CT: JAI.

Zentall, S. S. (1993). Research on the educational implications of Attention Deficit Hyperactivity Disorder. *Exceptional Children, 60,* 143–153.

Zentall, S. S., Falkenberg, S. D., & Smith, L. B. (1985). Effects of color stimulation and information on the copying performance of attentional problem adolescents. *Journal of Abnormal Psychology, 13,* 501–511.

7 Antecedent Interventions

Antecedent interventions involve attempts to alter the environment for children with ADD so that desirable, prosocial behaviors are more likely to occur and, conversely, undesirable behaviors are less likely to occur. Thus, efforts are directed toward change *before* the problem presents itself, a technique consistent with the sage advice to close the barn door before the horse gets out. In common practice too much emphasis is placed on consequence interventions (to be discussed in chapter 8) and too little on antecedent interventions.

This chapter first discusses the antecedent intervention having perhaps the greatest impact on the child with ADD: whether the child will be taught in a regular or a special class. Next discussed will be a number of accommodations relating to the structure of the regular classroom: organizing classroom space, establishing roles for others, establishing classroom rules, managing time, managing materials, and handling student requests for assistance.

The discussion of classroom structure is based on work by Dr. Stan Paine and his colleagues (Paine, Radicchi, Rosellini, Deutchman, & Darch, 1983). Although this work is not directed specifically toward children diagnosed with ADD, much of it applies to this population. The following assumptions are central in this regard:

1. All children can be taught, and their behavior can be managed.

2. Children's learning failures must be seen as teaching failures, not as an inability of the child to learn.

Similarly, their failure to behave appropriately must be seen as a failure to structure their environment sufficiently for successful conduct.

3. Low-performing children need to be taught at a faster-than-average rate, not at the same or a slower rate than other children; likewise, programs designed to teach them need to be more highly structured, not less. (Paine et al., 1983, p. 6)

REGULAR VERSUS SPECIAL CLASS PLACEMENT

The decision whether a child's needs will be met by placement in a regular classroom, resource room, or self-contained special education class should be made on a case-by-case basis. A number of factors are involved in the placement of a child with ADD. The extent of disturbing behaviors plays a part, with the acting-out child being more likely to be placed in a self-contained special education class. Other factors include the child's social relationships with peers, the presence of learning disabilities, and level of academic functioning. A final consideration is whether or not the classroom teacher is willing and/or able to make modifications in teaching style to accommodate the child.

Special education placement has a number of advantages:

1. The teacher/student ratio is much lower, allowing for smaller groupings of children.

2. Educational accommodations are more easily implemented.

3. Physical movement is tolerated to a greater degree.

4. Curricula can be highly individualized.

5. The child can be matched with peers having similar difficulties.

6. Certain interventions (e.g., tokens or rewards) can be used with the entire class, thereby not causing any particular child's differences to stand out.

Despite these advantages, many arguments exist for maintaining the child with ADD in a regular classroom setting. Basically, these center around the social stigma attached to a special education placement and the need to normalize the child's school experience. Often, a team-teaching effort is employed by the regular classroom teacher and the special education teacher to keep the child in the regular classroom.

George, Jacky, and Dennis were each maintained in a regular classroom, but the issue of whether they belonged in special education classes was raised in each case. Careful consideration was given to the potential costs and benefits of each choice, with George's case debated with the greatest intensity. Regular classroom placement was possible in part because in each situation a teacher believed this option was in the best interests of the child.

ORGANIZING CLASSROOM SPACE

The first suggestion for all teachers who want to increase their effectiveness in teaching children with ADD is to give serious consideration to the organization of the physical environment. Three objectives can be met by attending to this factor: decreasing noisiness and disruptions, increasing positive interactions with other students, and increasing on-task behavior.

One of the first interventions to consider is the arrangement of desks. Desks are usually arranged in either clusters or rows (see Figure 7.1). Cluster seating promotes student interaction and is therefore not recommended for the child with ADD. It is preferable to use row seating. This reduces the chances that the child's need for increased stimulation will negatively affect nearby classmates. It is also highly desirable to locate the child with ADD in the front row, center, because most teacher attention is directed toward the person who occupies this position. It will be easier to observe and monitor the child's behavior if he or she sits in that seat. Teachers should also consider the classmates who sit next to the child with ADD. It is best to surround the child with peer models who are well behaved and who show a high rate of on-task behavior.

Another structural intervention is to provide a physical space in the classroom in which activity is permitted. This will allow the child with ADD a break from classwork and the opportunity to move legitimately from one place to the other. Many teachers have arranged such a space, complete with materials and activities that are enjoyable and provide additional practice in academic and/or social skills.

ESTABLISHING ROLES FOR OTHERS

Providing roles for others in the classroom is a structural strategy that has the potential to help the child with ADD not only with de-

Figure 7.1   Row Seating Versus Cluster Seating

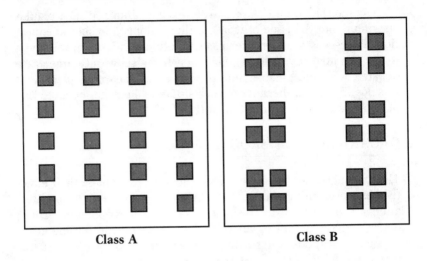

Class A   Class B

portment but also with academics. If a teacher is fortunate enough to have an assistant in the classroom it is helpful to specify the exact responsibilities of this person with regard to the child with ADD. One teacher developed a daily schedule for her assistant to follow (see Table 7.1).

However, most teachers do not have an assistant. These teachers may find that using other students as peer teachers is successful. Generally, the two areas the child with ADD needs the most assistance with are completion of classwork and social behavior. A peer can be designated a "study buddy" who would check the student's work for completion and accuracy, just as an assistant teacher would. It may be a good idea to have the children reverse roles, allowing the child with ADD to check the work of the study buddy. This will keep the children on an equal footing.

Identifying a "social buddy" to help the child with ADD in the cafeteria, at recess, and/or upon arrival at school may reduce the probability of negative exchanges with other students, initiated by the child with ADD to obtain attention. Encouraging telephone contact between these students can facilitate social interaction and give the child with ADD a resource from which to obtain information on missed or forgotten class activities.

Table 7.1   Sample Timetable for Teaching Assistant's
Supervision of Child with ADD

Task	Time	Interaction
1. Arrival	8:45 A.M.	Greeting, review of morning schedule
2. Group discussion	9:00–9:30 A.M.	Monitoring behavior (praise for on-task, ignore for off-task)
3. Independent work	10:00–10:30 A.M.	Monitoring behavior (praise for on-task, ignore for off-task)
4. Lunch	12:15 P.M.	Review lunch rules and consequences
5. Cooperative learning	1:30–2:10 P.M.	Review rules, give verbal prompts and praise
6. Departure	3:00 P.M.	Check homework materials

ESTABLISHING CLASSROOM RULES

Every teacher recognizes the importance of classroom rules. Rules serve four important functions in the classroom. First, rules communicate expectations. Children are clear on what they need to do and how they need to act in order to succeed. Second, rules help establish fairness as a doctrine in the classroom. Fairness is a concept significant to all children—they need to know that they will be treated fairly and that the teacher does not apply consequences indiscriminately. Rules that apply to everyone in the class communicate this important message. Third, the consistent application and enforcement of rules encourage children to demonstrate consistent behavior themselves. Finally, rules serve as cues for the teacher in responding to various behaviors.

The four functions served by rules apply to any child in any classroom. They are especially important for the child with ADD. The development of rules for the child with ADD should be considered in relation to the child's Stimulation Comfort Zone (SCZ) and

Attentional Bias to Novelty. For example, a rule might specify that upon completion of independent seatwork, a student and her social buddy can play a quiet game together (with prior teacher approval, of course) in a designated area.

Principles of Rule Development

The following principles of rule development should be observed:

1. The number of rules should be kept to a minimum, perhaps no more than three or four for the young child and perhaps five or six for the adolescent.

2. The wording should be simple but specific (e.g., "Use indoor voice" rather than "Respect others").

3. Rules should be stated positively whenever possible. Rules convey information, and a negative rule (e.g., "Do not hit") communicates what *not* to do but does not convey what to do. The admonishment "Don't think of pink elephants" usually results in that very thought. In the same way, stating rules negatively may actually encourage the negative behavior. Moreover, a long list of "Do nots" generally results in unpleasant feelings.

4. Rules should be situation specific. For example, it may be appropriate to raise one's hand to speak in class during a test, but at other times it may be appropriate to speak without raising one's hand. The classroom teacher may need to make these subtle differences explicit for the child with ADD.

5. Rules should be publicly posted. It is not a good idea to have children rely on memory or, even worse, repeat rules over and over again. Write out the rules for a given situation (e.g., playground rules, rules for lining up) and display them prominently. Doing so facilitates compliance.

Participation in Rule Making

The major concept that guides the establishment of rules is "owner-ship." It is clear now that the perception of having some input into the development of a rule enhances one's commitment to adherence to the rule. For this reason, the classroom teacher might begin by asking children what rules are needed for a given situation. Following is an exchange between a special education teacher and a group of children with ADD.

Teacher: Before we go out to the playground, we need to have some rules. Why do we need to have some rules?

Child 1: We need rules so we won't get into trouble.

Child 2: Yeah, and so we can go out again tomorrow.

Teacher: I'm going to ask you to come up with the rules you think are important, but the rules have to be specific and they have to be positive.

Child 3: "Don't cut in line."

Teacher: That is specific, but is that positive or negative?

Child 3: I think that's negative.

Child 1: How about "Wait your turn in line"?

Teacher: Very good. That is both specific and positive.

Child 4: I got one. "Pleasant talk," like the rule we have in class.

Teacher: OK. Any others?

Child 5: "No hitting."

Child 3: That's a negative.

Child 2: How about "Keep your hands to yourself"?

Teacher: You did a very good job coming up with the rules. Who would like to make a poster of these?

All the children participated in making the poster. The teacher decided to put up a new poster each Monday for a weekly review. This satisfied the children's need for novelty and helped maintain attention.

Making Rules Stick

The saying "It's easy to talk the talk, but it's hard to walk the walk" certainly applies to rules. The difficulty is not in knowing the elements of good rules but in making the rules stick. To help with adherence, conduct a Rule Review Procedure (RRP) prior to the anticipated problem situation rather than waiting until after the problem has occurred. For example, if your class is going to watch a film with another class, it is best to involve the child with ADD (or the entire class) in a discussion of the rules, using the concepts described earlier. With continued rule adherence, the frequency with which the RRP needs to be used should be decreased. However, there may be times when the RRP needs to be reintroduced, especially after weekends, vacations, or long absences due to illness.

Second, establish positive consequences for rule adherence. One teacher used a prearranged hand signal (a thumbs-up). For other children, more powerful positive consequences may be necessary. These strategies will be covered in chapter 8.

Finally, use a Teaching Interaction Procedure (TIP) for rule violation. At the first—not the second or third—rule violation, respond immediately by removing the child quietly from the group. The TIP is designed to help the child learn cause-and-effect relationships, to internalize the rule, and to strengthen compliance. The procedure is illustrated in the following dialogue.

Teacher: What rule did you just break?

Child: I don't know.

Teacher: You didn't keep your hands to yourself. Can you tell me what rule you broke?

Child: I was bad?

Teacher: No, you weren't bad. You didn't keep your hands to yourself. What rule did you break?

Child: Keeping my hands to myself?

Teacher: That's right! What do you need to do when you go back to the group?

Child: I need to keep my hands to myself.

Teacher: Very good! I'll be looking to see you do that and when I do I'll give the thumbs-up sign, OK?

Child: OK!

MANAGING TIME

Time management is an important antecedent intervention. Once wasted, time can only be made up at the expense of something else.

For example, if language arts is scheduled daily from 10:00 to 10:35 A. M., then the instructional time is 35 minutes per day or 175 minutes per week. Assuming the classroom teacher adheres to this schedule, the amount of instructional time available for the child with ADD will be determined by transitional time (i.e., the amount of time it takes to shift from one activity to another) and on-task time (i.e., the amount of time allotted minus the amount of time staring out the window, talking to a peer, going to the bathroom, looking under the desk for a paper, sharpening pencils, etc.).

Jacky was observed by her classroom teacher, Mr. Q., during the 35 minutes of language arts for 5 consecutive days. Choosing a simple recording procedure, Mr. Q. used a stopwatch to record all the time Jacky was observed to be on task. He started the stopwatch while Jacky was on task and stopped it whenever Jacky was off task. Mr. Q.'s data indicated that Jacky spent only 41 minutes out of a possible 175 minutes on task. This amounted to a little more than 8 out of the 35 minutes per day allotted to language arts!

The first step in managing time is to identify those periods during the course of the day that are problematic. These will usually break down into transition times and on-task times. The second step is to identify a resource person to assist the child in time management. This may be a teaching assistant, a peer, an older student, an adult volunteer, or the teacher. The third step is to decide how to make the timing element novel so that it challenges and interests the child. Because children with ADD are attracted to novelty, making a game out of a boring activity by using a timer or some other "gimmick" has the potential to increase performance.

One teacher created a game in order to motivate a small group of children who had difficulty staying on task during independent seatwork. The game was presented to the students as follows.

Teacher: Today we are going to play a game to help us pay attention.

Child 1:   How do you play?

Teacher: First, let me tell you what you can win. At the end of the day all those who win can go outside for an extra 15 minutes of free time. Those who don't win will continue to work with me in class.

Child 2:   Cool! How do we win?

Teacher: I'm going to pass out these sheets of work for you to do at your desk for the next 20 minutes.

> You need to do your work quietly, stay in your
> seat, and raise your hand if you need help. This
> timer will be set to go off at different times, and
> when it does whoever is following all the rules
> gets one point. Everyone who has eight or more
> points is a winner. Any questions?

Child 3: Do we get any second chances?

Teacher: No second chances, but the timer is going to go
off 10 times.

The results of the game were dramatic. The children stayed on task
at a much higher rate. However, the teacher was aware of the children's Attentional Bias to Novelty and knew she would likely have to
change the game at some point in the future in order to hold their interest.

Another teacher developed a way to address the problem of excessive time lost to transitions: Ms. Jones had three students diagnosed with ADD in her class. These three children often had a great
deal of difficulty shifting from one activity to another. Problems
would develop in getting their belongings together, moving from one
part of the room to another quickly and efficiently, and getting set-
tled to begin the next task. Because the class was learning about
graphs and charts, Ms. Jones decided to build an intervention around
this lesson. She announced that she was going to begin keeping track
of transition times from one activity to the next. She selected a student each day to time the class, making sure that each child had a
chance to be the "official timer." The official timer would start as soon
as Ms. Jones gave the cue and would stop when the last child had
successfully completed the transition. Ms. Jones then created a chart
on the chalkboard for the children to copy into their notebooks. Each
day's times were added to the chart. Once the class had been charting
for a few days, Ms. Jones had the children graph the data using a
linear and then a bar graph. This intervention was highly successful.
Not only did it teach charting and graphing skills, it also did not single out any particular child's behavior as problematic.

MANAGING MATERIALS

Another important antecedent intervention involves addressing the
difficulties children with ADD have managing school materials—
books, papers, pencils, notes, homework, and so on. Comments fre-

quently made about these children are "He's so disorganized"; "She'd lose her head if it wasn't attached to her shoulders"; "He can never seem to find anything"; and "I don't know why she didn't turn in her homework—I saw her do it last night." In the classroom, students with ADD often find objects in their desks far more interesting than the teacher's presentation. They may be observed playing with a matchbox car or spending 10 minutes going through the papers crammed into the corner of the desk searching for yesterday's incomplete assignment. Whether they find the mess in or under their desks more novel than the lesson being presented or the mess is a result of the previous day's impulsivity, the end result is the same—a failure. Managing materials is a skill that has to be directly taught to many children. Rather than taking it for granted that every child already possesses these skills, it is better to accept the fact that some may need instruction in how to organize themselves.

It may be helpful to have the child with ADD clear his or her desk of all extra materials, then create a storage space (e.g., a plastic box) for materials away from the desk. This storage space should be visible at all times and should have both writing implements and clearly marked and color-coded folders for schoolwork. The folders should have specific labels, such as "Work to do in school," "Work to do at home," "Completed work in *(subject),*" and "Graded work." The child should have an opportunity to check the storage space in the morning, the middle of the day, and then again at the end of the day. Because the space is highly visible, the teacher has ample opportunity to do spot-checks and give feedback. Teachers who have found this successful have recommended that such strategies be used at home as well.

HANDLING REQUESTS FOR ASSISTANCE

Many children with ADD call out or wander around the classroom for a variety of reasons. Often, these behaviors occur so many times per day that the teacher and/or classmates are distracted and irritated. If the child is engaging in these behaviors because he or she needs the teacher's assistance, it will be necessary to help the child get that assistance in more appropriate ways or to cope with difficult or boring material independently.

One strategy many teachers have found useful involves finding a way for the child with ADD to get attention by using a silent signal that allows the child to keep working while waiting. Some teachers have used a pencil with a flag on it stuck in a piece of clay, whereas others have used a printed "help" sign the child can place on his or her desk. In the beginning, the child with ADD may find using the signal or sign fun and therefore may use it to excess. Once the novelty wears off, the child will likely use it more appropriately.

In summary, antecedent interventions are preventive by nature. By considering the strategies and issues described in this chapter, the classroom teacher will be better able to minimize the chance that a problem will occur or that a small problem will grow into a large one. Indeed, antecedent strategies should not be reserved for use with children with ADD, but rather have the potential to be of benefit to all children. As such, they should be in the repertoires of all teachers.

References

Paine, S. C., Radicchi, J., Rosellini, L. C., Deutchman, L., & Darch, C. B. (1983). *Structuring your classroom for academic success.* Champaign, IL: Research Press.

8 Consequence Interventions

Consequence interventions, or interventions that attempt to modify behavior through the application of positive or negative consequences, are perhaps the oldest and most commonly used interventions in classroom settings for all children. Consequence interventions are effective for the student diagnosed as having ADD as well. However, certain characteristics of the disorder must be taken into consideration when designing consequence interventions for this group. This chapter discusses basic principles in consequence interventions, identifies potential pitfalls in their use, describes special considerations relating to motivation and children with ADD, and offers general guidelines for successful use of these methods.

CONSEQUENCE PRINCIPLES

Consequences are of two types: positive and negative. Positive consequences increase the frequency, intensity, and/or duration of a given behavior, whereas negative consequences decrease a behavior's frequency, intensity, and/or duration.

Positive Consequences

It is clear that positive consequences, when thoughtfully applied, can have a dramatic effect upon the behavior of students with ADD. Experience suggests that when positive consequences are immediate, frequent, salient, and rotated so as to avoid habituation, students with ADD may perform in school in a manner indistinguishable from their peers without the disorder.

Identifying reinforcers

The first step in designing an intervention based on positive consequences is to determine what consequences are actually reinforcing to the child (i.e., which consequences will strengthen a desired behavior). Tables 8.1 and 8.2 list common reinforcers for children and adolescents in the school and home settings.

Although a number of strategies exist for identifying consequences that are potentially reinforcing for a particular child, the best method may be to observe the child's actions. If a child is given free rein in a given setting, the teacher can observe behaviors that occur more and less frequently. The more frequent the behavior, the more reinforcing it is likely to be. For example, if Jacky is observed to spend more time wandering around the room than sitting at her desk during the time for independent seatwork, then, for Jacky, wandering around the room is more reinforcing than sitting at her desk.

Formal questionnaires can also be helpful in determining reinforcing consequences. A reinforcement inventory, when used as part of a structured interview with a student, can elicit valuable information as to potential positive consequences. Figure 8.1 shows a Reinforcement Inventory for Dennis. (A blank version of this inventory appears in the Appendix.)

The Motivation Assessment Scale (MAS; Durand, 1990) can also provide insight into potentially reinforcing consequences. For example, George often disturbed his third-grade class during independent seatwork by calling out, cracking jokes, or asking the teacher questions while she was involved with a small reading group in a corner of the classroom. The MAS indicated that the primary function of these behaviors for George was to escape classwork. George's teacher was able to use this information to develop a consequence intervention plan to increase completed work and decrease disruptive behavior. Specifically, the teacher divided George's work into smaller segments than for the rest of the class and allowed him breaks once he completed each segment. As an alternative to bothering the other students, George was allowed to spend his breaks in the computer corner with a peer and then return to his seat to complete more work.

Reinforcing consequences can also be identified through informal interviews with the child or the child's parents. It may be useful for teachers to question parents about the child's interests, preferred

Table 8.1   Sample Effective Reinforcers for School

Children

Having extra or longer recess
Helping the custodian
Being group leader
Fixing bulletin board
Going to the library
Running errands
Being hall monitor
Playing a game
Listening to records or tapes
Helping librarian
Sharpening pencils
Viewing films or videotapes
Being excused from homework
Partying
Getting a drink of water
Having choice of seat mate
Watching self on videotape
Having free time
Playing an instrument
Having story time
Participating in crafts activities
Having lunch with teacher
Being head of the lunchline
Making a videotape

Erasing chalkboards
Telephoning parent
Going to the principal's office
   on errand
Using stopwatch
Tutoring another student
Getting a good note to parent
Chewing gum in class
Getting positive comments on
   homework
Having picture taken
Getting stars or stickers
Being cafeteria helper
Getting badges to be worn
   all day
Demonstrating a hobby to class
Getting a special certificate
Being principal's helper
   all day
Having snacks
Getting free activity time
   (puzzles, games)
Getting a happy face on paper

Adolescents

Being group leader
Running errands
Playing games
Seeing films or videotapes
Playing an instrument
Making a videotape
Chewing gum in class
Having free activity time
Having an extended lunch
   period
Participating in school trips
Having the opportunity to
   improve grades

Wearing a baseball cap in class
Being in charge of class
   discussion
Serving as hall monitor
Listening to records or tapes
Having a homework pass
Tutoring another student
Demonstrating a hobby to
   the class
Developing a school radio show
Playing a video game
Being on a sports team
Being dismissed early from class

Table 8.2   Sample Effective Reinforcers for Home

Children

Social

Hugs	Pats on the back
Kisses	High fives
Verbal praise	

Privileges or activities

Dressing up in adult clothing	Eating out
Opening coffee can	Choosing the menu for a meal
Taking a trip to the park	Going someplace alone with
Helping make dessert	a parent
Playing with friends	Making a long distance
Feeding the baby	telephone call
Reading a bedtime story	Baking something
Having late bedtime	Planting a garden
Playing on swing set	Planning a day's activities
Going to the movies	Using tools
Spending the night with friends	Riding a bicycle
or grandparents	Using the telephone
Listening to the stereo	Wearing parent's clothing
Riding next to the window	Choosing television program
in a car	Being excused from chores
Going to a ball game	Going fishing
Making a home videotape	Camping out in the backyard

Material

Toys	Snacks
Pets	Own bedroom
Books	Clothing

Token

Money	Allowance
Stars on chart	Own bank account

Adolescents

Social

Smiles
Hugs
Winks
Verbal praise
Head nods

Thumbs-up sign
Receiving attention when
talking
Being asked for opinion

Privileges or activities

Having dating privileges
Getting driver's license
Reading
Having an extended curfew
Receiving car privileges
Staying up late
Staying overnight with friends
Having time off from chores
Dating during the week
Having the opportunity to
earn money
Selecting television program
Using the family camera
Choosing own bedtime

Participating in activities
with friends
Having a part-time job
Having friends over
Participating in dance or
music lessons
Redecorating own room
Rollerblading/skateboarding
Having additional time on
the telephone
Listening to the stereo
Making a trip alone on a bus
or plane

Material

Favorite meal
Clothing
Books
Radio
Bicycle
Electric razor
Watch
Makeup

Stereo
Jewelry
Guitar
Tapes or CDs
Own room
Personal television
Private telephone
Selecting own gift

Token

Extra money
Own checking account

Allowance
Gift certificate

Figure 8.1 Reinforcement Inventory for Dennis

Name _____ *Dennis* _____ Age/grade __*15/9th*__
Completed by _____ *M.J.A.* _____ Date _____ *9/20/93*

1. Who is your favorite adult at school?
   Mr. Salzman, my media teacher

2. What is your favorite school subject?
   Broadcasting

3. What are three things you most enjoy in school?
   Lunch

   My broadcasting class

   Goofing around

4. What school activity would you most enjoy doing with a friend?
   Hanging out at lunch

5. While in school, what would you like to do if you had a chance?
   Telling jokes

6. What school activity would you most enjoy doing with your teacher?
   Doing a comedy show in broadcasting

7. What is the best reward a teacher can give you?
   Letting me slide on my homework

8. What weekend activity do you most enjoy?
   Partying on Saturday night with my friends

9. If your teacher gave you free time to do anything you wanted to do in the classroom, what would you do?
   Sitting around telling jokes

10. Below is a list of privileges or activities that some students enjoy. Please circle the items you would like.

School

Being group leader
Running errands
Playing games
Seeing films or videotapes
(Making a videotape)
Chewing gum in class
(Having free activity time)
(Having an extended lunch period)
Participating in school trips
Having the opportunity to improve grades
Wearing a baseball cap in class

Being in charge of class discussion
Serving as hall monitor
(Listening to tapes or CDs)
(Having a homework pass)
Tutoring another student
Demonstrating a hobby to the class
(Developing a school radio show)
(Playing a video game)
Being on a sports team
(Being dismissed early from class)
Playing an instrument

Home

Having dating privileges
Getting driver's license
Reading
(Having an extended curfew)
Receiving car privileges
Staying up late
(Staying overnight with friends)
(Having time off from chores)
Dating during the week
(Having the opportunity to earn money)
Selecting television program
Using the family camera
Participating in activities with friends
Having a part-time job
Having friends over
Participating in dance or music lessons
Redecorating own room
(Rollerblading/skateboarding)
Having additional time on the telephone

Listening to the stereo
Making a trip alone on a bus or plane
Choosing own bedtime
Favorite meal
Clothing
Books
Radio
Bicycle
Electric razor
Watch
Makeup
Stereo
Jewelry
(Guitar)
Tapes or CDs
Own room
(Personal television)
Private telephone
Selecting own gift
Extra money
Own checking account
Allowance
Gift certificate

activities at home, and use of free time. For example, knowing that a child enjoys drawing or spending time with a friend in the same class can allow the teacher to arrange time for drawing or playing with that friend once the child has completed a certain amount of work.

The reinforcement hierarchy

The concept of a reinforcement hierarchy is helpful when attempting to develop an effective intervention plan. The more internal the reinforcement, the greater the personal responsibility, whereas the more external the reinforcement, the lesser the personal responsibility—and the more responsibility placed on the teacher. The goal in working with children with ADD is to move them up the reinforcement hierarchy to the point where they can reinforce themselves for a desired behavior.

BIOLOGICAL REINFORCEMENT. At the bottom of the hierarchy is biological reinforcement, such as food or drink. These reinforcers have been widely used with children having severe developmental disabilities such as autism or mental retardation, and their use is generally limited with children diagnosed as having ADD. This is not to say that food purchased with tokens has not been effectively used, but rather to suggest that most teachers will try to exhaust other possibilities before resorting to this basic type of consequence.

SYMBOLIC REINFORCEMENT. One step higher is the use of symbolic reinforcement, such as stars, stickers, points, tokens, and so on. These items have value only because they can be exchanged for desired objects, events, or activities on some prearranged basis. The concept of children's earning tokens for desired behavior and in turn using these tokens to purchase privileges has been used by legions of teachers.

ACTIVITY REINFORCEMENT. Activity reinforcement may be as common as extra recess or as unique as the opportunity to use a video camera. The idea of providing access to a high probability, preferred activity only after completion of a low probability, less preferred activity is known as the *Premack Principle* (Premack, 1959). This concept has been affectionately referred to as "Grandma's Law" or "You have to eat your vegetables before you can have your dessert." The principle may seem simple enough, but in practice it may be underutilized or distorted. Areas in which teachers may fail to use the principle correctly include distorting or ignoring the conse-

quence principles (e.g., providing 15 minutes of free time as a consequence for completing all classwork for an entire week) or not
incorporating them within the context of the five-stage model (e.g.,
using extra recess as a positive consequence for a student who feels
uncomfortable on the playground and actually prefers to stay with
the teacher rather than interact with peers). Finally, teachers may
fail to take into account the unique characteristics of ADD as they
relate to positive consequences (e.g., the comparatively rapid rate
with which rewards may lose their effectiveness or the need for more
frequent delivery of these consequences).

A very clever teacher, concerned about one student's difficulty
in staying at her desk to do independent seatwork, decided to develop an intervention plan to address this problem. After completing
the MAS and collecting baseline data, the teacher concluded that the
student generally went off task in order to move about physically.
The teacher held a sharing conference with the student and her parents, and the four of them developed a plan. They decided that the
student would do her independent seatwork while a 3-minute egg
timer was running. When the timer ran out, she was to take the timer
and her work, walk across the room to another designated seat, and
begin to time herself again as she continued to work. For a designated amount of time, the student was to continue this behavior,
moving between the two seats at 3-minute intervals. The plan was
highly successful.

SOCIAL REINFORCEMENT. One step above activity reinforcement is social reinforcement. This type of reinforcement takes the
form of adult attention, recognition, kind words, and other expressions of approval. Most children, including those with ADD, are motivated by social reinforcement. In fact, this may be the most powerful
tool in a teacher's repertoire. Unfortunately, social reinforcement as
a positive consequence is often overlooked or even misused. For example, if attention is reinforcing, paying a great deal of attention to
a child for behaving badly in class may result in strengthening the
very behavior a teacher wishes to weaken. It may not matter that the
attention takes the form of scolding or reprimands.

Social reinforcement often involves the giving of verbal or nonverbal attention. Verbal attention may consist of describing that
which is observed without evaluative comment (e.g., "Jacky, I see
you're sitting in your seat, you've completed three problems, and
you're working on the fourth one") or with evaluative comment (e.g.,
"Dennis, it was great the way you were able to wait your turn to
speak today"). Many teachers provide students with this type of so-

cial reinforcement already, but what some overlook is how easily this approach can be undermined by falling into the "zap trap." The zap trap is when the teacher habitually adds a criticism to even a positive evaluative comment (e.g., "George, you came into class, opened your notebook, and began doing the exercises all on your own. That was terrific! Now why can't you do that all the time? If you had done this yesterday, we would have had such a good morning. You wouldn't have been sent to the principal's office, your mother wouldn't have been called, and you wouldn't have had to miss the party. See, George, it's not so hard to be good, is it?"). In this example, the teacher may have felt the message was positive and encouraging, but George probably felt defeated. This type of interaction would eventually teach George to be careful of praise because criticism may follow. In fact, this technique would be more suitable if the teacher wanted to desensitize the student to praise: The technique of delivering praise and following the praise with a "zap" on a random basis would eventually result in the student's tuning out as soon as praising began.

Tone of voice is an important variable in delivering social reinforcement. Some teachers deliver social reinforcement, especially evaluative comments, in the same tone of voice they use for lecturing, questioning, or even reprimanding. Because the verbal reinforcement does not stand out, it may become just another stimulus to which the student does not attend. The teacher may need to deliver social attention in an exaggerated form, with a slightly raised voice, even sounding like a television game show announcer at times. There are exceptions to this rule, however. Some students with ADD may be embarrassed by the content of loud praise; others may be sensitive to the loudness itself. Teachers must experiment to identify what works best for which child. The same caution applies to nonverbal social attention. Squeezes on the shoulder, pats on the back, "high fives," or even "love taps" on the arm may be very positive to one student but unimportant or even aversive to another.

Motivating the student with ADD through social reinforcement has a major advantage because, in spite of the subtleties of its appropriate use, it comes naturally to many teachers. In addition, because it is used with many students who do not have ADD, it is unlikely to cause the child with ADD to stand out. Finally, because of its widespread use among educators, it is an intervention that can easily be continued as the child moves from teacher to teacher or grade to grade.

It is important to stress that social reinforcement should always accompany the use of other reinforcers lower in the reinforcement hierarchy. It is hoped that by pairing reinforcers in this way, eventually social reinforcement alone will motivate the student. If social reinforcement does become motivating, there is a greater likelihood that the desirable behavior will be transferred from one setting to another.

SELF-REINFORCEMENT. At the top of the hierarchy is self-reinforcement. Here the student delivers a positive consequence to himself or herself, either by virtue of the personal satisfaction derived from the act itself or through the delivery of self-talk (e.g., thinking, "I'm proud of myself"). Self-reinforcement motivates children to do work, follow classroom rules, share with others, and do all the other things adults expect. Students who function at this level are often described as independent, responsible, and mature.

Cautions in using positive consequences

It is a complex task to create a successful intervention based on positive consequences for the child with ADD. One problem may arise if the positive consequences on which the intervention depends are artificial or unfamiliar to others in the school environment. In such a case, it is unlikely that the intervention will be applied on a long-term basis, especially if the child will be changing teachers from subject to subject or from year to year. Implementing such a program—even if initially effective—may become very labor intensive. Basing interventions on positive consequences that already exist within the school environment will help ensure maintenance of gains.

Teachers may also experience difficulty if differential rewards for children with and without ADD are used. Many teachers believe offering differential rewards is unfair. Even if teachers feel special treatment is warranted, parents and/or the children themselves may not share this perspective. Fairness is an issue that has long been misunderstood. It is often assumed that fairness means treating all children the same. The reality is that there are many circumstances in which children are treated differently—for example, in the case of the student in a wheelchair who is permitted to use the elevator and the student with a learning disability who is permitted to take an untimed test. It can help people understand differential treatment if the concept of fairness can be framed as giving each child what he or she needs to succeed.

Negative Consequences

A great deal of misunderstanding exists with regard to the use of negative consequences with children in general and with students with ADD in particular. It is important to understand that negative consequences are a natural part of life that cannot be avoided. The young child who touches a hot stove will experience the natural aversive consequence of pain. Depending upon the child's intelligence, memory, gross motor skills, and impulsivity, repetition of the behavior will eventually teach the child to avoid touching the hot stove. In most situations these natural negative consequences are perhaps the best teacher of all. However, many circumstances exist in which the natural aversive consequences for a given behavior (e.g., playing baseball on a heavily trafficked street) are too dangerous, too inconsistent, or too delayed to be allowed. Given that negative consequences are fairly good regulators of human behavior, it is better to arrange these consequences effectively and safely in a controlled environment than to allow the child to learn naturally in what may turn out to be a much harder way.

There are two conditions under which negative consequences *should* be applied following an inappropriate behavior. In the first case, the inappropriate behavior produces an immediate positive consequence—for example, when a student with ADD aggressively grabs a toy from another child. The mere fact that the aggressor is now in possession of the desired object reinforces the aggressive behavior. In the second case, the inappropriate behavior is potentially dangerous to the child or to others—for example, when a child runs down a school corridor.

However, negative consequences should not be the first or only strategy the classroom teacher uses. Rather, they should follow or be implemented in conjunction with positive consequences incorporated within the context of the five-stage model of behavioral assessment (see chapter 4). In any behavior change effort, a reward intervention should precede a punishment intervention. The basic problem with punishment as a consequence is that it conveys information about what is inappropriate without conveying information about what is appropriate. One can leave it to chance that the child will discover the correct alternative; however, it is far more effective to integrate positive consequences with negative consequences.

The three most common negative consequences used in the classroom with students who have ADD are planned ignoring, reprimands, and response cost. Two more types of negative consequence are especially effective with children diagnosed with ADD: boredom punishments and effort punishments. Given their Attentional Bias to Novelty (see chapter 6), children with ADD will be particularly responsive to negative consequences that involve boredom or that require repetitive, sustained effort.

Planned ignoring

Planned ignoring involves doing just what it suggests—ignoring undesirable behavior. In cases in which it has been determined that an inappropriate behavior (e.g., calling out) is being reinforced by teacher attention, no matter how negative, planned ignoring would call for the withdrawal of attention when the behavior occurs. However, if the target behavior is not maintained by teacher attention, then planned ignoring will be ineffective. For example, in one class, a student enjoyed doing an impression of Michael Jackson's "moonwalk" on top of his desk. His classmates were delighted by this behavior and took to screaming and clapping whenever he did it. It was assumed that the student was engaging in the behavior to gain the teacher's attention, and she was instructed to use planned ignoring. In spite of her consistent efforts, the moonwalks did not decrease in frequency, intensity, or duration. In fact, it was not the teacher's attention that was maintaining the behavior but that of the boy's peers. Once it was determined that the attention of the peer group was actually maintaining the behavior, the rest of the class was encouraged to ignore the misbehavior. Then and only then did the inappropriate behavior begin to weaken.

An important but often overlooked point about planned ignoring is that whenever attention or any other type of reinforcement is removed the student will intensify the behavior in an attempt to gain back what has been lost. This intensification must be anticipated; giving in only serves to teach the child with ADD to be more persistent and more inappropriate.

Reprimands

Reprimands have been a mainstay of teacher discipline. Recently, questions have been raised about the effectiveness of reprimands for certain children. For those motivated to gain teacher/peer attention, public reprimands actually may serve to strengthen the very behavior the teacher desires to weaken. For this reason, although effective for the majority of children, reprimands must be used cautiously with a student diagnosed as having ADD. Private reprimands, audible only to the child with ADD, seem to be more effective.

Response cost

The negative consequence most investigated with regard to children with ADD is response cost. This intervention involves a penalty, usually the loss of points, upon the occurrence of certain specified negative behaviors, such as calling out, disturbing others, or running in the halls. Response cost is generally viewed by teachers as both effective and easy to administer.

As is true for other negative consequences, a concern with response cost is that the only feedback given to the student is for undesirable behavior. As mentioned earlier, it will be more effective to use negative consequences for inappropriate behavior in conjunction with positive consequences for appropriate behavior.

Boredom punishments

Boredom punishments are basically of three types: sit and watch, sit and think, and in-school suspension.

SIT AND WATCH. This consequence involves identifying a specific target behavior—for example, rocking back and forth in one's chair during circle time. If the child engages in the behavior, the instructor should calmly point out and label the misbehavior for the child. The child should then be removed to a sit-and-watch chair for a brief period of time (from 2 to 5 minutes). He or she should be asked to observe how the others engage in the desired behavior (e.g., "Ethan, you need to sit and watch how the other children keep all four legs of their chairs on the floor"). The rest of the class should be praised for behaving appropriately (e.g., "Jamal, I like the way you and Martha have your chairs on the floor").

Once the sit-and-watch time has elapsed, the teacher should conduct a brief Teaching Interaction Procedure, or TIP, with the child. The TIP is an attempt to establish greater awareness and increase compliance by asking the child "Why are you in sit and watch?" and "What do you have to do now?" The interaction concludes with praise when the child demonstrates the desired behavior.

This type of boredom punishment is based on the central assumption that the student with ADD wishes to be in the group. Sit and watch has the added benefit of using the positive modeling of peers to influence the student's behavior.

SIT AND THINK. A more restrictive type of boredom punishment is sit and think, a procedure identical to sit and watch except that the child is removed from the area and does not have the opportunity to observe the class. This more restrictive procedure should be used only if sit and watch proves ineffective. As with sit and watch, the effectiveness of sit and think is based on the assumption that the child wants to be with the group. To increase the likelihood of this desire, positive consequences for participation, such as praise or points exchanged for back-up rewards, need to be abundant and powerful.

IN-SCHOOL SUSPENSION. Older students with ADD, especially at the middle and high school levels, are subject to the disciplinary code in effect for the entire student body. Typically, students who are successful in school, want to be thought of in a positive light, and are concerned about parental approval are highly motivated to avoid any type of school suspension. Adolescents with ADD, however, often view an out-of-school suspension as a "vacation," especially if there is little or no adult supervision at home. It is far more effective for a district to establish an in-school suspension policy, in which attendance is required and work must be completed in isolation from the rest of the student body. While in-school suspension is in effect, the student must earn his or her way back into classes by accomplishing certain predetermined tasks.

Effort punishments

Because persistence of effort is difficult for many youngsters with ADD, negative consequences that demand work of some sort are highly unpleasant. Among these are the effort punishments of simple correction, overcorrection, and positive practice.

SIMPLE CORRECTION. Simple correction means that, upon the occurrence of a misbehavior, the child with ADD must stop what he or she is doing and restore the environment to its original condition. Imagine a student with ADD impulsively running into the classroom and knocking into a row of desks, sending notebooks and papers flying everywhere. Simple correction would require the child to stop, set the desks back in place, and replace the notebooks neatly in their original positions.

OVERCORRECTION. Overcorrection requires that the child not only restore the environment to its original condition but also make it better than it was. For example, a student might be required to perform 100 hours of community service for writing graffiti on school walls. Not only must the student clean the walls, he must also spend additional time cleaning the building and maintaining the grounds.

POSITIVE PRACTICE. This effort punishment requires that the child practice the correct form of action repeatedly. For example, a student who throws her leftover lunch into the trash from across the room might be required to get the lunch, return to her seat, get up, walk to the trash can, drop it into the garbage, pick it up again, return to her seat, and repeat the entire process for however long the instructor directs (perhaps 20 times or for 15 minutes). It should be decided in advance when the positive practice should take place (i.e., immediately or after school). Positive practice is highly aversive in the effort it demands. In addition, it requires the child to practice the desired response.

CASE EXAMPLES: POTENTIAL PITFALLS IN CONSEQUENCE INTERVENTIONS

In designing consequence interventions for students with ADD, teachers must take into consideration the unique aspects of the disorder. Without such consideration, even programs with a high likelihood of success for students without ADD run the risk of failure. In the following case examples, the interventions failed for this reason.

George

George had significant academic difficulties compounded by the problems he had staying in his seat and completing assigned work. His third-grade teacher, Ms. A., decided to implement a sticker program that would provide George with a reward upon his completion of each academic task during the school day. Ms. A. discussed her plan with George, and he appeared eager to participate.

In the beginning, improvement was rapid—George left his seat much less during class and completed much more of his classwork. He would regularly bring his completed work to Ms. A., who would give him a sticker of his choice. Most of the time, George put his sticker on his shirt to show the class he had completed the assignments. Ms. A. was thrilled with the outcome of her intervention and felt George was doing considerably better in her class.

Approximately 2 weeks after the intervention began, George started completing fewer assignments. He received fewer stickers, but he didn't seem to care. Ms. A.'s frustration was intense as the program began to lose its effectiveness.

Jacky

Jacky was very slow completing her classwork. At times, in fact, she wouldn't do it at all. Mr. Q., her fourth-grade teacher, felt that Jacky's problem was a lack of motivation. He decided to implement a reward system for the completion of classwork and homework. Mr. Q. and Jacky decided that she would receive a token at the end of each day if all her work was completed. At the end of the week, if Jacky had collected a token for each day (a total of five tokens), she would be allowed to select a reward (e.g., an eraser, pencil, pen) from a "goody bag" provided by Mr. Q.

Although Jacky seemed excited about the plan and did complete more classwork, even after several weeks she was unable to obtain the tokens necessary to get the reward. On her best weeks, she was able to obtain only three out of the five tokens. Over time, Jacky became discouraged. The initial gains were short-lived.

Dennis

Dennis had considerable difficulty with tardiness and truancy and, as a result, was doing very poorly in most of his high school classes. His guidance counselor met with him to discuss the importance of developing a plan to address these problems. Together, the counselor and Dennis identified two primary reasons Dennis stayed in school: to attend his broadcasting class and to make social contacts during school hours. The counselor then developed a contract built on these incentives. The first condition was that if Dennis failed to improve his grades and decrease his tardiness and truancy, he would be unable to sign up again for another media class. The second condition was that if Dennis missed any classes during the school week, he would be required to attend Saturday morning detention. Dennis and his counselor wrote up the contract with the terms agreed upon by both parties.

The next day, Dennis skipped his geometry class and was required to serve Saturday detention. As time went on, the tardiness, truancy, and grades did not improve, and Dennis was spending every Saturday in detention.

These three cases of failed intervention are fairly typical—consequences are applied without taking into account the unique characteristics of ADD. George's case illustrates how easily habituation occurs for children with ADD. The life span for a reward program such as the one described may be only a few weeks. After that period, the child may no longer be interested in receiving the same reward. For Jacky, the reward offered was too delayed. The tokens at the end of each day provided only limited feedback for her daily progress. In addition, the 5-day wait for a tangible reward did not motivate her sufficiently to complete the assigned classwork. The approach attempted with Dennis failed because punishment alone is rarely powerful enough to help a youngster with ADD attend to the requirements of the environment. In addition, the punishment chosen was too delayed.

ADD AND MOTIVATION

To understand the difficulties illustrated in the preceding case examples, it is necessary first to understand that motivation in children with ADD does not equal inspiration or will power. Admonishing children with ADD to try harder will only intensify frustration for all concerned. Motivational problems in this group are neurobiological—that is, they originate within the central nervous system and specific brain areas. Because of this motivational deficit, children with ADD are likely to do poorly in environments where rewards are weak, delayed, infrequent, and ordinary. Needless to say, those are the characteristics of many classroom reward systems. It is no wonder that the classroom poses the greatest area of difficulty for children with ADD.

The prominent researcher and clinician Dr. Russell Barkley (1990) has reconceptualized ADD as a motivational deficit disorder. This new perspective attempts to explain why children have attentional problems in some situations but not in others. Barkley suggests that the degree of motivation determines the level of participation across situations and is primarily responsible for sustaining attention to tasks. He further suggests that responses to environmental consequences (e.g., delayed rewards or punishments) may be impaired for children with ADD and that this accounts for many of the behavioral difficulties they encounter in classroom settings.

Barkley further postulates that the motivation of children with ADD, or their responsiveness to rewards and punishments, is different from that of their peers. One possibility is that these children are insensitive to delayed rewards, preventing long-term rewards from exerting control over behavior. Although they profess a desire for the future positive consequences, children with ADD do not experience the promise of the reward as strong enough to deter them from indulging in a behavior that will satisfy them now, even if they know it is "wrong." Thus, the classroom program with the reward on Friday may work for the majority of students but may not be very effective for students with ADD.

Children with ADD are also very sensitive to immediate rewards. They have been routinely observed to be highly motivated when an immediate reward exists. When given a choice between a large, delayed reward or a small, immediate reward, these children will choose the latter. They seem to be ruled by the moment.

As seen with George, many children with ADD lose interest in rewards. Rewards that work at first may lose their effectiveness over time. The teacher who observes this deterioration on a daily or weekly basis may rightly suspect a growing insensitivity to the type of reward provided, explained by the Attentional Bias to Novelty. Because novelty is so important to the child with ADD, what is reinforcing this week may be boring next week. This presents a real challenge to the classroom teacher, who must be ready to inject novelty whenever necessary.

In addition, rewards for children with ADD must generally be greater in magnitude. The stickers and stamps that serve to motivate other students often fail to do so with many children who have ADD. Such children desire a great deal of stimulation, and rewards for them need to be chosen with this fact in mind.

Children with ADD may also be different in terms of their response to punishment. Some believe that children with ADD may be insensitive to punishment, as evidenced by the fact that they seem less responsive than other children to reprimands, scoldings, cross looks, and even detentions. Parents often testify that they only gain control by use of an escalating spiral of punishments in which they end up screaming at or even spanking their children. The problem with such methods is that they work only in the short term—more and more extreme measures are required to control the problem behavior. The same is true for the teacher's use of reprimands, scolding, and detentions. A thoughtful intervention involving the individualized use of both positive and negative consequences will be far more successful over a long period of time.

GUIDELINES FOR USING CONSEQUENCES

Repeated attempts and failures to intervene by controlling consequences will be confusing, frustrating, and disheartening for teacher and student alike. For this reason, the following general guidelines should be observed. First, it is important to understand the causes and nature of ADD and to avoid subscribing to the many myths and misconceptions about the disorder (see chapter 2). Second, careful consideration should be given to the child's developmental level. In order for interventions to be successful, the teacher must recognize the limitations of cognitive and social development during the pre-operational stage, stage of concrete operations, and stage of early formal operations, as discussed in chapter 3. Third, before using a consequence intervention, it is best to structure the classroom by employing appropriate antecedent interventions (see chapter 7). Finally, any consequence intervention must be undertaken according to the five-stage model, as described in chapter 4.

Whenever consequence interventions are used, the following guidelines will help ensure success:

1. When the child with ADD displays either appropriate or inappropriate behavior, the teacher's feedback should be immediate. The child can then learn to rely on this feedback for help in adapting.

2. Because the child with ADD can work for a shorter period than his or her classmates, consequences must be delivered more frequently.

3. Incentives must also be richer and more alluring, and it is necessary to rotate reinforcers frequently. (For example, when George's interest in the sticker program abated, it might have been worth Ms. A.'s time to introduce new rewards to prevent habituation.)

4. Positive consequences should be tried before negative consequences—and negative consequences should never be used alone but always in conjunction with appropriate positive consequences.

References

Barkley, R. A. (1990). *Attention Deficit Hyperactivity Disorder: A handbook for diagnosis and treatment.* New York: Guilford.

Durand, V. M. (1990). *Severe behavior problems: A functional communication training approach.* New York: Guilford.

Premack, D. (1959). Toward empirical behavior laws: Positive reinforcement. *Psychological Review, 66,* 219–233.

9 The School Environment Learning Program

The School Environment Learning Program, or SELP, has been used successfully with hundreds of children ranging from elementary to high school age. Participating students have been variously diagnosed by mental health professionals as having ADD, Oppositional Defiant Disorder, and/or Conduct Disorder. Within a school setting, they have been classified as Perceptually Impaired, Neurologically Impaired, or Emotionally Disturbed. The program has also been successful with children considered underachieving but within the normal range of adjustment.

Briefly, SELP is a structured program based on control of consequences. It focuses on four school behaviors: following class rules, completing classwork or participating in class (whichever is appropriate), completing homework, and getting along with other students. Teachers assign points for a student's performance on these various behaviors; the student can then exchange these points for rewards or privileges.

Importantly, the attainment of rewards rather than the avoidance of punishment is the program's primary focus. The problem of habituation to consequences is anticipated through the use of a "reward menu," or variety of rewards. These may be either school-based (e.g., extra time on the computer) or home-based (e.g., use of the telephone in the evenings). Although response cost is a component of SELP, the program's main goal is to help students obtain as many privileges as possible. SELP also employs frequent and immediate feedback in the form of the teacher's informal evaluation at the end of each class period. This consequence is either reinforcing or aversive according to whether or not the scores obtained entitle the student to basic and/or special privileges.

The SELP program is designed to incorporate the principles of the five-stage model of behavioral assessment (see chapter 4). First, the student's problems are clearly pinpointed through the identification of the four target behaviors. Second, measurement is undertaken prior to implementation to obtain an assessment of the student's preintervention functioning. Third, the program is designed to fit the student by allowing for modification of the basic definitions of the target behaviors to ensure that they are personally relevant. Fourth, data are collected on a continual basis so that modifications can be made when necessary. Finally, evaluation of the program is made simple through the use of chart and graphs.

The program requires an active commitment on the part of teachers and parents, for they are the ones who will actually carry out the procedures, in consultation with a school psychologist, principal, guidance counselor, or outside therapist. Initially, the program may seem complex, but with time the procedures become automatic. If carefully administered, SELP can dramatically improve school performance for students with ADD.

SELP PROCEDURES

Blank copies of the SELP Daily Scorecard, Reward Menu for Home/School Privileges, and Weekly Record Sheet, referred to in this section, appear in the Appendix. The case examples subsequently presented show how each of these forms is used.

1. Each school day is divided into time periods. These divisions can be by time of day (e.g., 9:00 to 9:30 A.M.) or by specific academic subject (e.g., reading, arithmetic).

2. Teachers use a Daily Scorecard to rate the child on four target behaviors: follows class rules, completes classwork or participates in class, completes homework, and gets along with other students. The specific criteria for assigning points in each category are as follows.

   Follows class rules
   4 = All rules followed for the entire period
   2 = Most of the rules followed for the entire period
       (e.g., runs to get in line)

0 = Breaks at least one major rule (e.g., pushes another
  student)

Completes classwork or participates in class (whichever is
appropriate)
4 = Completes 80 to 100% of classwork/good participation
2 = Completes 60 to 79% of classwork/average participation
0 = Completes less than 60% of classwork/poor participation

Completes homework
4 = Completes 80 to 100% of homework
2 = Completes 60 to 79% of homework
0 = Completes less than 60% of homework

Gets along with other students
4 = Gets along with every student
2 = Gets along with most students
0 = One or more major incidents with another student

If a certain category is not applicable (e.g., completes
homework), the teacher notes this by marking an X.

3. Initial scoring takes place privately for 5 days, without
   informing the child. This establishes a baseline or pretreatment
   measure to ensure that the program begins at the student's
   actual level of performance.

4. Teachers and/or parents meet to establish *basic privileges* at
   school and/or at home. These consist of approximately four
   activities that are reinforcing for the child and that can be
   controlled either at home cr at school (e.g., going out to play
   with friends, bedtime, television privileges, free time in class,
   computer time). The basic privileges are listed on a Reward
   Menu for Home/School Privileges.

5. The child must earn a predetermined number of points in
   order to obtain basic privileges. This number is the baseline
   number of points plus 10. For example, if after a 5-day period
   of private record keeping the child's baseline is 20 points per
   day, then the number of points required for the child to earn
   basic privileges is 30 points per day.

6. At the end of each day the student and teacher (or parent)
   enter the total number of points earned. If the student has
   earned the requisite number of points, basic privileges will be
   available during the remainder of the day at home or at school
   the following day. At this time each day, the student has an

opportunity to discuss his or her performance. The teacher (or parent) gives feedback about the achievement of good ratings, reviews skills the student employed to get good ratings, and develops plans that will result in the student's progress. The goal is to help the student improve performance.

7. If the student earns more points in a day than are needed to obtain basic privileges, these extra points are deposited into a "savings account" and can be used to purchase *special privileges*. Special privileges, determined in advance, might include a sleepover with a friend, a weekend night out with friends, an extended curfew, extra time on the classroom computer, extra gym time, and the like. These privileges are also noted on the Reward Menu.

8. All points required to earn basic privileges must be used for basic privileges. This means that the student cannot decide to forego spending points for basic privileges in order to use them to purchase special privileges.

9. If the student fails to earn the points needed for basic privileges, the points earned that day are automatically lost. They do not apply to points already in savings.

10. If all privileges occur only at school, then points in savings can be used to purchase special privileges only when basic privileges have been earned for 2 consecutive days. If all privileges occur only at home, then points in savings can be used to purchase special privileges only when enough points have been earned in school to earn basic privileges. If privileges occur in both the school and home settings, then the rules are as follows: The student may earn special privileges at home after earning basic privileges at school for a single day; however, the student must earn basic privileges in school for 2 consecutive days before gaining special privileges in school.

11. When the program is designed for both home and school use, basic privileges are free on weekends.

12. If the program includes both home and school, the purchase of special privileges on weekends will be allowed only if the student has earned basic privileges every day of the school week.

13. Every 2 weeks, all points are totaled and a new basic privilege average is established. The goal is to challenge the student to improve and work toward more adaptive behavior.

CASE EXAMPLE: DENNIS

Dennis, the high school sophomore whose case has been discussed throughout this book, experienced two types of difficulty in school. First, he had content-based problems in organization, spelling, and reading. He also had the behavioral problems of inattention, disruptive behavior, tardiness, and truancy.

As discussed in chapter 8, Dennis's guidance counselor had already tried a response cost intervention. According to the terms of a contract both had agreed upon, Dennis would not be permitted to sign up for another media class if his grades did not improve. In addition, he would be required to serve detention on Saturdays every time he skipped a class. Unfortunately, this plan did not work well. The negative consequences were too delayed to inhibit Dennis's problem behaviors, and the agreement included no positive incentives for alternate behaviors.

After this failure, the guidance counselor consulted with Dennis's psychologist. Together, they decided to implement the SELP program. The guidance counselor felt SELP would help all parties concerned accurately monitor Dennis's performance and provide appropriate feedback on his behavior. The intervention was also approved by the school administration, Dennis's teachers and parents, and Dennis himself. In a sharing conference conducted in the guidance office, the counselor, parents, and all of Dennis's teachers met to go over the ground rules.

Each teacher, using the SELP Daily Scorecard, then privately evaluated Dennis on the four target behaviors listed (see Figure 9.1). This baseline data provided a "behavioral X-ray" prior to intervention. At the end of this baseline period, the guidance counselor collected the scorecards and tallied the number of points Dennis earned each day. The resulting daily average was used as the starting point for intervention. Figure 9.1 shows that Dennis earned only 46 points during a single day of baseline assessment. His average for a 5-day period was 48, not much better than his earnings for the single day shown.

Figure 9.2, the Reward Menu for Home/School Privileges, lists Dennis's basic and special privileges and the number of points required to earn them. Dennis participated in the selection of special privileges, with the final decision resting with school personnel and parents.

Because teachers' signatures were required on the Daily Scorecard, Dennis was required to attend classes regularly in order to earn

Figure 9.1   Dennis's Daily Scorecard During a Single Day of Baseline Assessment

Name _____ Dennis _____ Date _____ 3/25/93 _____

Please rate this student on his or her performance in your classroom in each category listed. Use the following scale:

4 = Excellent
2 = Fair
0 = Poor
X = Not applicable

Category	1	2	3	4	5	6	7	8	9	10	Total
Follows class rules	O	2	2	2	4	O	2	4	2		18
Completes classwork or participates in class	O	2	2	2	4	2	2	O	O		14
Completes homework	X	O	2	X	X	O	O	2	O		4
Gets along with other students	O	2	O	2	2	O	O	4	O		10
Teacher's initials	RF	MA	NS	SG	MA	DS	DW	SP	RT		
Total	O	6	6	6	10	2	4	10	2		46

Comments

Figure 9.2   Dennis's Reward Menu for Home/School
              Privileges

Name _____ *Dennis* _____ Date _____ *3/29/93* _____

Basic privileges	Points required
1. *Going to have morning coffee with classmates*	
2. *Using Walkman during school*	
3. *Using skateboard to and from school*	*48*
4. *Using the telephone during the evenings*	

Special privileges	Points required
1. *Homework pass*	*30*
2. *Holding comedy show on Fridays*	*30*
3. *Going out on Friday and Saturday nights*	*20–30*
4. *Renting a video*	*20*
5. *Rides to activities by parents*	*25*
6. *Sleepover at friend's*	*30*
7. *Making a video at school*	*30*
8. *Extended curfew*	*20*
9.	
10.	
11.	
12.	

---

points. In addition, Dennis had the opportunity to review his scores
daily with the guidance counselor and his parents, thus providing
him with specific feedback about his behavior and increasing his motivation.

Dennis's Weekly Record Sheet (see Figure 9.3) summarized his
performance over that period of time. The guidance counselor met
with Dennis to go over his weekly progress and to troubleshoot problems to ensure that Dennis would earn his basic privileges in the

Figure 9.3 Dennis's Weekly Record Sheet

Name: Dennis
Week beginning: 5/24/93
Points required for basic privileges: 88
Points carried over from previous week: 42

Day	Points earned	Points spent	Savings
Monday	96	88	50
Tuesday	112	88	74
Wednesday	68	0	74
Thursday	82	0	74
Friday	94	88+20 (going out)	60
Saturday	Basic privileges free	20 (going out)	40
Sunday	Basic privileges free	0	40

Note: On Wednesday and Thurday, Dennis earned fewer than 88 points, the total required for basic privileges. As a result, he was not allowed to spend any points for either basic or special privileges, and his balance in savings remained the same as it had been on Tuesday.

future. Every 2 weeks, Dennis's weekly performances were reviewed, the number of points Dennis needed to earn basic privileges was increased, and new privileges were added. Formal meetings of the counselor, Dennis, and his parents were also held at that time to address problems and evaluate progress.

Although at first the counselor acted as an external monitor, eventually Dennis became the primary monitor of the SELP program's effectiveness. He was able to receive and act on the feedback from his teachers. Figure 9.4 graphs his progress through the first and last 4 weeks of the program. As the graph shows, Dennis made good progress.

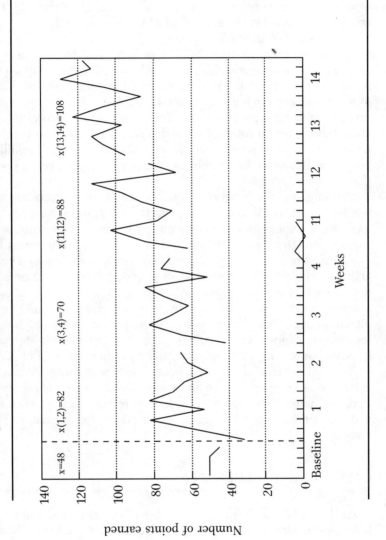

Figure 9.4   Dennis's Progress for the First and Last 4 Weeks of SELP

In Dennis's case, the guidance counselor coordinated the program and ensured that the information was collected, the consequence principles were understood, and that new consequences would be added continually to maintain Dennis's motivation. The counselor attended to the issue of social validation by obtaining feedback from each of Dennis's teachers.

Dennis's participation in SELP was motivated by his desire to enter his junior year with his peers and to continue signing up for media electives. His skills, resources, and energy indicated an ability to work with the program. However, he did have a tendency to give up as soon as he experienced a setback, such as poor scores in one class. Dennis would think, "I blew that class, so there's no point in trying now." This type of thinking tended to create a self-fulfilling prophesy. This and other problems were addressed in meetings with the guidance counselor.

Throughout the program, Dennis's counselor, instructors, and parents recognized that it was important for him to socialize and be an active member of the school community. The guidance counselor worked with Dennis and his teachers to focus on the four target behaviors outlined and to avoid setting tasks beyond his developmental abilities. All parties concerned were provided literature addressing the difficulties adolescents with ADD experience. Other educational accommodations were also implemented to facilitate Dennis's completion of classwork. Among others, these included breaking longer lessons into shorter segments, providing clear instructions both verbally and in writing, developing an organizational checklist for Dennis's assignments and required books, and permitting Dennis to exhibit work completed in an alternative format (e.g., oral presentation, videotape). The end result was a more empathic intervention with reasonable yet challenging expectations for overall performance.

CASE EXAMPLE: MICHELLE

Michelle, age 9, had been having severe difficulties in school for at least a year. Although Michelle was at grade level academically, she was having problems following classroom rules, paying attention, completing classwork, turning in her homework, and getting along with other children. Most recently, Michelle was also beginning to show evidence of "fresh talk" and was teasing other children excessively. Her failures were considered serious enough to warrant numerous discussions between her teacher, Ms. S., and her parents, Mr.

and Mrs. J. Ms. S. was very concerned because she felt that Michelle was unhappy and therefore inattentive. She found that she often had to repeat herself to get Michelle to listen. When repetition failed, Ms. S. resorted to reprimands, warnings, detentions, and parent conferences. Nothing seemed to work.

The school psychologist conducted interviews with Mr. and Mrs. J., Michelle, and Ms. S. Psychological testing and a learning evaluation were used to gather more information. A sharing conference including all the parties resulted in the decision to implement the SELP.

A 5-day private baseline was undertaken without Michelle's knowledge, using the Daily Scorecard. Figure 9.5 shows that Michelle earned 42 points during a single day of baseline assessment. Over the course of the entire 5-day period, Michelle's points earned ranged from a high of 52 to a low of 10, with an average of 28.

In collaboration with Ms. S. and with Michelle's input, Mr. and Mrs. J. developed a Reward Menu for Home/School Privileges for Michelle (see Figure 9.6). Mr. and Mrs. J. and Ms. S. determined that Michelle needed to earn 38 points per day (28 plus 10) to earn all her basic privileges. Although they were prepared for a less-than-enthusiastic response, much to their surprise Michelle was eager to gain special privileges and seemed to look forward to the start of the program.

Michelle did quite well for the first few days of the program, earning all her basic privileges. However, Mr. and Mrs. J. were wise enough to know that this was the "honeymoon." Shortly thereafter, Michelle had a terrible day. She had a major temper tantrum, tore up all the recording forms, and ran away from home for a few hours. When she returned, her parents calmly told her that she needed to tape the forms together and that they were going to continue to follow the program.

Over the next few months, Michelle began to show steady improvement, as recorded on Weekly Record Sheets (see Figure 9.7 for an example). Occasionally, setbacks did occur, but they were less frequent, less intense, and of shorter duration than before the SELP was implemented. Figure 9.8 illustrates Michelle's progress during the first and last 4 weeks of the program. She was gradually weaned from the program by entering a phase of self-monitoring whereby she rated her own behavior and checked her ratings against those of her teachers.

Mr. and Mrs. J. continued to use the program for the remainder of the school year. At the start of the new school year both parents noted significant improvements in Michelle's overall behavior and did not feel a need to use the SELP again.

Figure 9.5   Michelle's Daily Scorecard During a Single Day of Baseline Assessment

Name _____ *Michelle* _____   Date _____ *2/9/93* _____

Please rate this student on his or her performance in your classroom in each category listed. Use the following scale:

4 = Excellent
2 = Fair
0 = Poor
X = Not applicable

Category	1	2	3	4	5	6	7	8	9	10	Total
					Class period						
Follows class rules	2	0	2	0	0	0	4	4	0		12
Completes classwork or participates in class	2	2	2	0	X	4	2	4	0		16
Completes homework	X	2	2	X	X	X	2	X	X		6
Gets along with other students	0	2	0	0	0	0	2	2	2		8
Teacher's initials	SS	SS	MR	SS	SS	MR	MR	BA	RC		
Total	4	6	6	0	0	4	10	10	2		42

Comments

Figure 9.6 Michelle's Reward Menu for Home/School Privileges

Name _____ *Michelle* _____ Date _____ *2/15/93* _____

Basic privileges	Points required
1. *Going out to play after school*	
2. *Watching television, playing videogame*	38
3. *Choice of snack in the evening*	
4. *Being read to before bed*	

Special privileges	Points required
1. *Getting an extra bedtime story*	10
2. *Spending the night at a friend's house*	25
3. *Going to McDonalds*	50
4. *Getting a new doll from the toy store*	50
5. *Staying up an extra half-hour on weekends*	15
6. *Chore pass*	15
7. *Calling cousin or friend long distance*	20
8. *Using Mom's make-up*	15
9. *Going to the movies*	50
10. *Choosing meal for dinner*	20
11. *Going to video store for tape*	25
12.	

Figure 9.7   Michelle's Weekly Record Sheet

Name   _Michelle_

Week beginning   _4/26/93_

Points required for basic privileges   _76_

Points carried over from previous week   _45_

Day	Points earned	Points spent	Savings
Monday	88	76	57
Tuesday	94	76+50 (new doll)	25
Wednesday	74	0	25
Thursday	82	76	31
Friday	90	76	45
Saturday	Basic privileges free	25 (night at friend's)	20
Sunday	Basic privileges free	0	20

Note: On Wednesday, Michelle earned fewer than 76 points, the total required for basic privileges. As a result, she was not allowed to spend any points for either basic or special privileges, and her balance in savings remained the same as it had been on Tuesday.

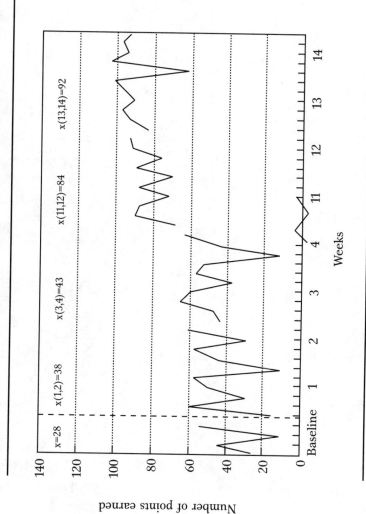

Figure 9.8 Michelle's Progress for the First and Last 4 Weeks of SELP

10 Cognitive-Behavior Therapy: The Russian Connection

In the 1920s the prominent Russian scientist Lev Semenovich Vygotsky provided the impetus for the cognitive-behavioral movement with children. While observing children at early stages of language development, Vygotsky (1962) developed a paradigm concerning the relationship between the internalization of dialogue (i.e., talking to oneself) and the development of thought or cognition. He concluded that children used self-talk to mediate behavior and to solve problems. Vygotsky's view was in striking contrast with that of his contemporary, Piaget, who believed children's self-talk was simply imitation of others' language.

Proponents of cognitive-behavior therapy (CBT) assume that the difficulty regulating behavior seen in the child with ADD stems from a flaw in the development of the child's self-talk skills. Predictably, CBT is designed to foster self-regulatory skills through the use of self-talk or self-statements. Children with ADD are taught to employ a variety of verbal problem-solving strategies to guide, direct, and focus their behavior. These strategies help children with ADD talk themselves through new or difficult situations.

CBT training is often done by a child's parents and/or a private therapist. Unfortunately, in many cases the teacher does not take part in the child's training. As the central figure in the child's life for a major portion of the day, the teacher establishes activities, sets the tone, and makes the majority of classroom decisions (i.e., selecting instructional materials and determining classroom organization). As such, the teacher is in a unique position to facilitate self-instruction in the setting where it is most needed—the school environment. The child may also be more comfortable and receptive if the self-instructional program includes the classroom teacher as a primary change agent.

CBT requires that teachers learn to modify their interactive style with children diagnosed as having ADD. Recently, there have been a number of books and package programs that train teachers to employ CBT (e.g., Asher & Schleser, 1988; Braswell & Bloomquist, 1991). Among these approaches to self-instruction, Faded Rehearsal Self-Instruction, developed by Dr. Donald Meichenbaum (Meichenbaum & Goodman, 1971), and Directed Discovery Self-Instruction, developed by Dr. Robert Schleser (Asher & Schleser, 1988; Schleser, Armstrong, & Allen, 1990; Schleser, Cohen, Meyer, & Rodick, 1984; Schleser, Meyer, Cohen, & Thackwray, 1983), appear to offer the greatest promise.

FADED REHEARSAL SELF-INSTRUCTION

Faded Rehearsal Self-Instruction (FRSI) is an approach that has been found most effective with children at the preoperational stage of development (generally from ages 2 through 6). The program depends on a certain degree of verbal facility; thus, in practice, the lower end of this age range will be about 4 years. Given that children with ADD may not develop as quickly as their same-age peers without the disorder, the upper end of the range may actually extend to ages 8 or 9.

This self-statement, problem-solving model involves six steps:

1. Stop! Identify the problem.

2. Think of some possible plans.

3. Choose the best plan.

4. Implement the plan.

5. Check to see if the plan is being followed.

6. See if the plan works and self-reinforce.

The teacher helps the student learn this six-step process over several brief meetings. Below is an example of an actual case involving George, age 8, and his third-grade teacher, Ms. A. These meetings took place during the lunch period approximately every other day over the course of 2 weeks.

Meeting 1: Developing Interest in Behavior Change

The purposes of this introductory meeting are (a) to heighten the child's interest in developing alternative learning habits, (b) to provide strategies for the child to learn to control behavior, (c) to show the child how to make plans to get along better in school, and (d) to teach the child to use self-talk to guide and direct behavior. Self-talk is described as a natural event: "We all talk to ourselves."

The teacher begins by explaining to the child that they will be working together to learn and practice new ways of planning for and solving daily problems at school. This conversation, ideally one-on-one, should be nonjudgmental, in order to foster open communication, and should be adapted to each individual child. The goal is for the child to identify and explain the need for a specific plan to deal with current problems. These problems may include noncompliance, classroom disturbances, or incomplete assignments. It is also helpful to discuss the effects of the child's behavior on classmates. The teacher and the child then evaluate the child's personal, social, and academic strengths and the willingness of both individuals to work together to help the child become more successful.

Ms. A.:   I asked for a meeting today because I thought maybe we need some time to start a new way of making sure you get your work done.

George: OK.

Ms. A.:   We've had some trouble getting along in the past, and there have been some problems with your getting your work done, so I wanted to try a new idea. You can talk to yourself with this new idea. Talking to yourself can be a way of helping you get your work done.

George: OK.

Ms. A.:   Do you talk to yourself now?

George: Sometimes I talk to myself about things I want to do.

Ms. A.:   Maybe this time we'll talk about ways of slowing yourself down so that you can do better in school. OK? We're going to do things to help you put your ideas in order and figure out ways of thinking things through so you don't jump ahead.

George: All right.

Ms. A.:   Good. Maybe you could tell me some of the things you have had trouble with in school. What kinds of things do I keep talking to you about?

George: Reading.

Ms. A.:   Reading? I'm going to write these ideas down so we can remember them.

George: I jump out of my seat and run around.

Ms. A.:   Does that help you get your reading done?

George: No.

Ms. A.:   No. What does it do to the other kids?

George: It makes them want to jump out, too.

Ms. A.:   (Laughs.) So that's not helping getting the reading done.

George: No.

Ms. A.:   OK. What other things get in the way of getting your work done?

George: Well, sometimes I want to be the first one done.

Ms. A.:   What happens when you do your seatwork?

George: I get mad.

Ms. A.:   You get mad? When you get mad, what happens? What do you do?

George: I have to calm myself down and get back to work.

Ms. A.:   How do you calm yourself down?

George: I try to remember to do my work.

Ms. A.:   So, do you get out of your seat then, too?

George: Yes.

Ms. A.:   What happens? Does your work get done?

George: No.

Ms. A.:   No. So what happens then?

George: I get in trouble.

Ms. A.:　You get in trouble. Would you like to get your work done?

George:　Yes.

Ms. A.:　OK. Some of the things we're going to learn are ways to help you so that work gets done and you get to do some other things. Do you lose out on things because your work isn't done?

George:　Yes. I get detentions, notes sent home, and stuff like that.

Ms. A.:　Can you think of anything else that gets in the way of getting your work done?

George:　No.

Ms. A.:　How about talking sometimes? Does that come from having a hard time getting your seatwork done?

George:　Yes.

Ms. A.:　Good. These are things that are hard for you. What about some of the things that you are good at?

George:　Arithmetic.

Ms. A.:　You're good at arithmetic. What kind of arithmetic?

George:　Using my ruler.

Ms. A.:　Using your ruler? Good. What else?

George:　Measurement.

Ms. A.:　How about adding and subtracting?

George:　Yeah. I'm pretty good at that, too.

Ms. A.:　So, arithmetic is good. Anything else that you feel good about?

George:　No.

Ms. A.:　Well, what do you think about trying something new so that you can get your work done and get to do other things in class?

George:　I would like that.

Ms. A.:   OK. What we're going to do is set up a plan so
          that you can start being able to talk to yourself
          and be able to concentrate on your work a little
          better. It will help you relax and slow down and
          concentrate on your work.

George: OK.

During this meeting the teacher also explains that there will be
a need to monitor the child's behavior during the course of the
school day.

Ms. A.:   We have to think of a way we can keep an eye on
          how much work you start getting done using your
          new plans. What do you think may be a good way
          to keep track?

George: (Shrugs.)

Ms. A.:   Let me tell you what I mean. One of the things
          I can do is watch you and look for changes in
          your behavior such as how well you're doing
          remembering to talk to yourself. How does that
          sound?

George: OK.

Ms. A.:   Also, I could keep a checklist of how you're doing.
          I can keep it on my desk to track your progress.

George: OK.

Ms. A.:   How about if you keep a checklist? What do you
          think that would be like? What would you do?
          What would you check off?

George: I'd check off what I did.

Ms. A.:   You'd check off what you did and whether you
          finished something?

George: Yeah.

Ms. A.:   OK. And you know what we could do after that?
          We could make a graph so you could see whether
          you had a good day or a bad day and how much
          work you got done.

George: OK.

Meeting 2: Evaluating the Child's Current Behavioral Choices

With the child's cooperation, the teacher next discusses the situations in which the child has difficulties, exploring all the potential consequences for each identified problem behavior. The teacher then has the child identify the potential changes that will occur as a result of self-talk. Together, they brainstorm different types of self-statements that students without ADD might use to guide and control their behavior. Speaking slowly and distinctly, the teacher then verbalizes potential self-statements that might be of use in regulating problem behaviors.

> Ms. A.: I'm going to go over the behaviors you talked about as being problems. One of them is reading because that is when you sometimes get out of your seat and jump around. Also, you talked about your seatwork being frustrating, and that gets you into trouble as well. You also brought up talking in class, and that gets the other kids going. Finally, getting your classwork and homework completed is sometimes a problem for you, isn't it?
>
> George: Yeah.
>
> Ms. A.: So those are the things we'll be taking a look at. Let's go back to reading for a second. When you jump up and run around, what happens?
>
> George: Nothing.
>
> Ms. A.: Nothing happens?
>
> George: No.
>
> Ms. A.: What do the other children do?
>
> George: The kids get out of their seats.
>
> Ms. A.: Do you like the fact that other kids want to get up, too?
>
> George: Yes—I mean, no.
>
> Ms. A.: What happens if all this starts?
>
> George: I get my name on the board, and the other kids get mad at me.

Ms. A.: Yes. That's called a consequence. That's one of the things that happens because you are not doing your reading. And if you did your reading and sat in your seat, how do you think everyone would feel?

George: Happy.

Ms. A.: Yes, I think so. How about your seatwork? What if you sat down, concentrated, and talked yourself through it and did your seatwork? What would happen?

George: It would be a lot better.

Ms. A.: What consequences happen when you don't do your seatwork?

George: Well, you get mad at me, my mom gets mad at me, I have to do more work at home, and I don't get to play or watch television.

Ms. A.: So, then it doesn't end up as much fun, does it?

George: No.

Ms. A.: What happens when you get your work done?

George: You say, "Good work," and everybody is happy.

Ms. A.: All right. What about talking in class? What happens when you talk in class?

George: You get mad at me.

The dialogue continues in this fashion by reviewing each identified problem and its consequences. The interaction then shifts to identifying self-statements that children without ADD might make.

Ms. A.: Let's think about other kids. They can stay in their seats, right? What do they say to themselves to help them sit in their seats?

George: I don't know.

Ms. A.: What might they say?

George: Beats me.

Ms. A.: You know what, we'll think about some of the things you could say, and you could think about whether they might say them. Do you think they might tell themselves to slow down?

George: Yeah.

Ms. A.: Do you think they might say to themselves to stop and take a look at what they are supposed to be doing?

George: Yeah.

Ms. A.: They might do that. I don't know if they do that, but do you think that might help you?

George: Yes.

Ms. A.: OK. Let's write some of these things down.

Meeting 3: Making Helpful Plans

The teacher and the child, pretending that a problem is occurring, evaluate the child's behavioral options. The teacher invites the child to imagine that he or she is in the classroom, to discuss temptations and feelings, to explore scenarios, and to think about the means by which conflict and its unpleasant consequences can be avoided.

Ms. A.: Now we're going to talk about plans. Do you know what plans are?

George: When you think about things you are going to do.

Ms. A.: That's right. Why are they important?

George: Beats me.

Ms. A.: What if you don't have plans?

George: It could help you a lot more to tell you where you want to go and what you want to do.

Ms. A.: Good. That's exactly why we have plans. That's great. What we are going to do is help you choose a plan to help you when you are bothered by another child. Let's say your friend is bothering you and calling you names, and you are trying to get your work done. Let's play a brainstorming game. I'll tell you the rules. First, we take turns coming up with a plan. Second, we can't say whether it's a good plan or a bad plan until we're all done. Third, we have to try to be creative. Fourth, if you can't come up with a new plan you say, "I give up." The winner is the one with the last plan.

George: I could hit him.

Ms. A.:   You could move away.

George: Get a soundproof room.

Ms. A.:   Sit there and ignore him.

George: Tell him to shut up.

This process continues until all plans are exhausted. The teacher then guides the discussion to a review of each plan and its consequences.

Ms. A.:   What would happen if you moved away?

George: He'd still be talking, and I wouldn't hear him.

Ms. A.:   Would you get your work done?

George: Yes.

Ms. A.:   You would? How?

George: I would take my pencil and paper and go someplace else.

Ms. A.:   What would happen if you hit him?

George: He would tell on me, and I would get in trouble. I would tell on him, and everybody would get in trouble.

The discussion continues until the consequences of each plan have been identified, discussed, and evaluated. After the child chooses the best plan, the discussion focuses on how to implement it. George and his teacher picked an area in the classroom to be George's special place and established a signal (i.e., a printed sign on his desk) to indicate silently that he was using his plan. This provided a cue to Ms. A. to give George a silent reinforcer (i.e., a thumbs-up sign).

Meeting 4: Faded Rehearsal—Introduction to Self-Talk

In this meeting the teacher introduces a "script" to help guide the process of generating self-statements, explaining that the four questions that are the framework for the script help children learn to talk to themselves while they work on problems. The teacher then has the child repeat the entire script. During the dialogue, the teacher dramatically illustrates the process with enthusiasm and animated movements—for example, scratching one's head, looking at classwork, checking the room for the teacher, correcting a mistake, or applauding or patting oneself on the back. Doing so gains the child's interest and helps the child better understand the context and development of the process.

> Ms. A.: One of the other things you wanted to work on was sitting in your seat. Let's think of a plan for sitting in your seat. Let's pretend I'm getting real itchy. I want to get out of my seat. I can't wait until the lesson is over. But I've got a problem. We're in the middle of class. I want to get out of my seat and walk around, but I say to myself, "I'm going to solve this problem. I'm going to stay in my seat." What do I have to do? Well, first I tell myself to slow down and stay in this seat. OK?
>
> George: OK.
>
> Ms. A.: Maybe I'll just jump up out of my seat and go bother the other children.
>
> George: No.
>
> Ms. A.: No? I'm going to stay in my seat?
>
> George: Yes.
>
> Ms. A.: Then I'm going to wait and say to myself, "I need to work. If I jump up and bother the other children, I'm not going to get my work done, the teacher is going to get mad at me, I'm going to get in trouble, and then the other kids are going to talk. That's not going to work."
>
> George: No.
>
> Ms. A.: So maybe I should try not to jump out of my seat—stay in my seat like the other children. If I do that, I won't get in trouble and I'll get my work done. Is that right? Does that sound like a good plan? Do you think you could do that plan?
>
> George: Yes.

Ms. A.:   OK. I have a something here that has helped other kids, and it might work for you. I'm going to read this to you, and you can listen very carefully.

What's my problem? (Scratches head and wrinkles forehead.) I'm going to solve a problem about being able to stay in my seat. *What do I have to do?* (Shrugs shoulders and turns palms of hands upward.) I'd better stop (gives hand signal to stop), slow down, and think about what I have to do to solve this problem. Maybe I should try not jumping out of my seat and sit like the other children. This is going to be hard. I want to get out of my seat. But if I do that, I know what will happen. OK, first I have to sit squarely in my seat, face my desk, and put both feet on the floor. Let's try it. I'll turn my paper so I can write. I won't look at the other kids. I'll look at my paper and stay in my seat.

Am I using my plan? (Pats self on chest.) I'd better check and make sure I'm following my plan. I'm sitting squarely in my desk. My feet are on the floor. I have my pencil in my hand, and I'm not looking at the other children, and I'm doing my work. Yes, I'm following the plan.

How did I do? (Smiles widely.) I had a problem because I wasn't able to stay in my seat and do my work, but now I've stopped and thought, and I've come up with a good plan. I think this is a good job. You know what else I thought of? I'm not going to have as much homework because I'm going to get my work done in class. This really works! I did a good job!

Meeting 5: Faded Rehearsal—Step Two

In this step the teacher has the child pretend to be a character in the script while the teacher states each of the four steps of the process and has the child repeat the self-statements one at a time. The teacher encourages the child to listen carefully to the statements and to act out the corresponding behavioral gestures.

> Ms. A.: Now we're going to play the copycat game. I'm going to say something, and when I pause you'll have to repeat it. Ready?
>
> George: OK.
>
> Ms. A.: What's my problem? (Scratches head and wrinkles forehead.) I'm going to solve a problem about staying in my seat.
>
> George: What's my problem? I'm going to solve a problem about staying in my seat.
>
> Ms. A.: What do I have to do? (Shrugs shoulders and turns palms of hands upward.) I'd better stop (gives hand signal to stop), slow down, and think about what to do about this problem of staying in my seat.
>
> George: What do I have to do? I'd better stop, slow down, and think about what to do about this problem of staying in my seat.

Some children require a cue to respond after each step, such as a head nod or point of the finger. This pattern of teacher verbalization followed by child imitation continues through the remaining steps with liberal teacher guidance, support, and encouragement.

Meeting 6: Faded Rehearsal—Step Three

This step is characterized by the child's taking on greater responsibility as the teacher gradually fades cues and support. If necessary, the teacher helps by prompting with one or two words, providing only enough assistance for the child to generate the statements. The teacher begins by asking the child to state the first thing he should say.

> Ms. A.: Today I'm going to give you an opportunity to use self-talk on your own. I'm going to give you cue words, and this is a script that you are going to remember, just as if you were an actor. I'm going to start at the beginning. Are you ready?
>
> George: Ready.
>
> Ms. A.: OK. Remember the beginning? Let's go back. I'm going to solve . . .

George:	I can't remember it.
Ms. A.:	What kind of problem are you going to solve?
George:	Staying in my seat.
Ms. A.:	Say the whole thing yourself.
George:	I'm going to solve the problem of staying in my seat.
Ms. A.:	Good. What question do you ask?
George:	What do I have to do?
Ms. A.:	I'd better . . .
George:	I'd better stop and put my feet on the floor.
Ms. A.:	Let's go back a step. You did the first part beautifully. You're going to stop and slow down and think about it.
George:	I'm going to stop and slow down and think of a plan so I don't get out of my seat. Maybe I could get out of my seat.
Ms. A.:	But wait . . .
George:	But wait, that wouldn't work.
Ms. A.:	If I jump . . .
George:	If I jump out of my seat, the other kids will notice, and I will get in trouble. I will have more homework to do.
Ms. A.:	Maybe I should . . .
George:	Maybe I should sit in my seat and do my work.
Ms. A.:	Is that right . . .
George:	Is that right? If I do my work and don't bother the other kids and get my work done? Yeah, that's it.
Ms. A.:	And I won't . . .
George:	And I won't bother the kids, and I won't get in trouble.
Ms. A.:	Now I need to . . .

George: I need to stay in my seat and do my work without bothering the other kids. I have to put my feet on the floor and put my paper in front of me.

Ms. A.: So I'd better check ...

George: I'd better check to make sure I'm following my plan.

Ms. A.: So what do you do?

George: I put my feet on the ground and don't look at the other kids.

Ms. A.: And I'm going to ...

George: I'm going to do my work.

Ms. A.: Yes, I'm ...

George: I'm following my plan.

Ms. A.: I'm not ...

George: I'm not going to bother other kids.

Ms. A.: And I'm going to ...

George: I am going to do my work.

Ms. A.: I had a ...

George: I had a problem, but now I don't, and I won't get in trouble.

Ms. A.: I stopped ...

George: I stopped and thought about what to do.

Ms. A.: I did a real ...

George: I did a real good job.

The teacher concludes this meeting with extensive praise and encouragement.

Meeting 7: Faded Rehearsal—Step Four

As the process progresses the statements are repeated very quietly, in a whisper, so that no one will hear what is being said. The teacher, helping only when necessary, encourages the child to listen carefully to the self-talk and to perform all corresponding behaviors.

Ms. A.: I would like you to tell me everything you are going to do to help yourself remember to stay in your seat.

George: I'm going to solve the problem by putting my feet in front and doing my work, but first I have to stop and slow down and think about what I'm doing to solve my problem. I could bother the other kids, but that won't work. I will get in trouble. Maybe I could put my feet on the ground, put my paper in front of me, and do my work.

Ms. A.: I need to . . .

George: I need to do my work and not bother other kids. I'd better check my plan. I put my feet on the ground, and I'm doing my work.

Ms. A.: I'm following . . .

George: I'm following my plan, and I'm not going to jump around and bother the other kids.

Ms. A.: I had . . .

George: I had a problem about staying in my seat, but now it's solved.

Ms. A.: I did . . .

George: I did a good job.

Meeting 8: Faded Rehearsal—Step Five

This time the child's self-talk is unspoken. The child thinks each part of the plan through carefully while the teacher performs the corresponding gestures and the child copies them. The teacher monitors the child for the demonstration of the gestures that correspond to the self-statements.

Ms. A.: I want you to copy my gestures. Don't say anything out loud. Think about your plan and remember what you have been saying to yourself. (Gives hand signal to stop.)

George: (Repeats hand signal and thinks, "Stop! Identify the problem.")

Ms. A.:   (Points to head.)

George: (Points to head and thinks, "Think of some possible plans.")

Ms. A.:   (Looks puzzled, with finger on chin.)

George: (Finger on chin, thinks, "Choose the best plan.")

Ms. A.:   (Smiles.)

George: (Smiles and thinks, "Try it out." Acts out plan by holding the pencil, turning the paper, etc.)

Ms. A.:   (Smiles and gives herself a pat on the back.)

George: (Pats himself on the back and thinks, "See if it works and reward myself.")

DIRECTED DISCOVERY SELF-INSTRUCTION

The Directed Discovery Self-Instruction (DDSI) approach to self-talk (Asher & Schleser, 1988; Schleser et al., 1990; Schleser et al., 1984; Schleser et al., 1983) is appropriate for children at the preoperational stage of cognitive development and has been shown to be superior to FRSI for children who have achieved the concrete operational stage (generally from ages 7 through 11). As for the FRSI, the child's actual stage of development, not chronological age, will determine the appropriateness of the technique. Children with ADD may be 8 to 10 years old before they actually begin to think concretely.

In addition to using the teaching strategies used in FRSI, this approach involves leading the child through a conversation designed to create conflict in the child's thought process. Through Socratic dialogue with the teacher, the child discovers the self-statements to guide and direct his or her behavior. The teacher must constantly evaluate the information implicit in each answer. If an answer reflects a poor decision or an ill-conceived direction, the teacher then uses conflict or Socratic questions to guide the child to the desired response.

This approach helps the child develop his or her own problem-solving skills, rather than relying on the teacher to state explicitly each step of the problem-solving process. The teacher demonstrates that changes in a child's behavior can result from a naturally evolving, systematic process of teacher-child interaction.

Because the teacher's communications are framed as questions, this process places responsibiiity for the conversation squarely on the child. Only when there is no response should the teacher use didactic statements or questions that can be answered yes or no. By asking questions, the teacher helps the child achieve distance from the situation. The child must think about the question and choose whether and how to address it. In most cases, this will cause the child to stop an inappropriate behavior and start an appropriate one.

Questions such as "What happens when you continue to bother your neighbor?"; "What are you supposed to be doing now?"; "How does what you are doing now make you feel?"; or "What do your classmates think?" should be delivered in a calm and neutral tone. The intent is to have the child begin to think and respond spontaneously, as if in the specific situation. The child should be encouraged to participate in the dialogue; responses should not be dismissed as inappropriate, but rather challenged until they approximate what the teacher is seeking. At this early stage, the teacher must recognize the hazards of judging the child's responses harshly. A teacher might begin by saying something like "I'm interested in knowing how you think and feel, so don't worry about how you word it, just try and get your thoughts out." The teacher should acknowledge the child's response by rephrasing: "So what you're saying is, if you don't get your work done now, you'll have to do it at home tonight." This technique, used in the early stages of this interactional process, is dropped once the teacher is more comfortable engaging the child.

The specific goals for a teacher using DDSI are as follows:

1. To develop self-statements that a child would use to control behavior

2. To work toward incorporating these self-statements into the child's thoughts and behaviors

3. To acknowledge that the child has the required skills but needs to interact with someone else to practice them

4. To use questions that elicit the child's self-generated statements

5. To act as an environmental prompt for the child to engage in self-talk

6. To use modeling of one's own behavior to help the child view the desired behaviors

7. To ask conflict-inducing questions to guide the child to select acceptable answers

Part of this discovery procedure includes helping the child use clearer and more concise language to solve problems. The nine-step approach described next provides a road map to guide the classroom teacher's use.

Step 1: Defining the Problem

This step begins with open-ended questions designed to stimulate thought and inspire insightful responses. The child and the teacher should anticipate different types of self-statements that may be used to guide and control the child's behavior. The teacher may ask, "What do you think the problem might be?"

Conflict-inducing questions are used to develop goal-directed statements and to elicit acceptable responses. The teacher should ask an open-ended question concerning the problem. For example:

"Tyrell, what are we working on today?"

"Jacky, what types of things keep you from succeeding in your boardwork?"

"Dennis, what gets you into the most trouble with me?"

"Amanda, if you have a problem, what's the first thing you should tell yourself?"

Acceptable responses are ones that clearly identify the problem—the task the child needs to accomplish and the obstacles that must be overcome to do so. For example:

"I do not do all my homework."

"I do not listen to the teacher during lectures."

"I hit other children when I am mad."

"My problem is . . . "

Step 2: Getting Ready

The second step is to help the child develop self-monitoring statements in preparation for stopping and thinking about how to solve the problem. It is helpful to encourage the child to engage in the corresponding behavioral gestures (e.g., coming to a complete stop and scratching one's head to indicate thinking). The child may stop the behavior and state, "I better stop this and think about what I should be doing now." The teacher then uses conflict-inducing questions to guide the child toward an acceptable response:

"Tyrell, if you are making a plan, is it best to jump right in? What should you do first?"

"Jacky, when you get excited, is it easy or hard to think? How can you make it easier?"

Step 3: Generating Solutions

During this step, the teacher probes for solutions to the problem behavior. The child should devise one or more ways to solve the problem. The teacher may ask questions such as the following:

"Tyrell, tell me some solutions to that problem."

"Jacky, what can you do to make sure you listen to my lectures?"

"Dennis, what are some things you can do so that does not happen?"

The child, encouraged to think about the problem, may give an answer that touches on specific remedial actions:

"I should do my homework right after school before I watch television."

"Instead of goofing off I could do my work so I don't get in trouble."

"I need to check my work before I turn it in."

Step 4: Checking Ideas

By asking questions that elicit an evaluation of various behaviors, the teacher helps the child recognize the possibility that if the solution creates additional negative consequences, it will need to be modified:

"What can happen if you don't finish your homework?"

"What might happen if you yell during music class today?"

"What happens when you break class rules?"

The child might respond as follows:

"If I don't do my homework, I won't get to be hall monitor."

"If I yell in school, I will get a demerit."

"If I do not follow the class rules, I will have to stay after school."

Step 5: Eliciting Appropriate Strategy-Generating Statements

At this point the child may need to revise the strategy. The teacher helps the child state the need to prepare an alternative plan to fit the situation better. The idea is to have the child recognize that plans can have different outcomes in different situations. For example:

"What if you thought your plan was good, and it didn't work? What would you do?"

"If something doesn't work the first time, what do you do?"

Step 6: Checking for the Correct Solution

The teacher prompts the child to check the strategy to determine the appropriateness of the plan. The teacher wants the response to include statements about behaviors that will increase the child's ability to monitor his or her own behavior:

"How can you make sure you are following your plan?"

"How are you going to know if the plan is right?"

"What can you do before you use your plan so it will work?"

The child's responses should be specific:

"I need to stop and think about what I am doing."

"Am I paying attention?"

"I need to think it through again."

Step 7: Initiating the Strategy

The teacher, wanting to heighten the child's cognitive focus, prompts the child to state the decision to implement the self-instructional plan:

> "Tyrell, what is the problem?"

> "Dennis, what is a possible solution?"

> "Jacky, use your self-instruction."

> "Will a plan work if you don't use it?"

> "How are you going to go about starting your plan?"

Step 8: Monitoring Solution Implementation

The teacher prompts the child to determine whether he or she is following the plan:

> "Tyrell, how can you get back on track with your plan if you forget what you are doing?"

> "Jacky, did you ever do a problem wrong, even though you were sure you knew how to do it? How could you have prevented that?"

Step 9: Reviewing and Reinforcing

The teacher prompts the child to acknowledge completion of the plan:

> "What is the final thing you should do?"

> "What can you tell yourself when you have finished something and done a good job?"

Finally, the child acknowledges the need to review the plan, identifies the original difficulty, comments on the effectiveness of the solution, and compliments himself or herself for resolving the problem.

An example of a complete DDSI interaction between Tyrell, age 11, and his sixth-grade teacher, Mr. M., follows.

Mr. M.: What is it that you do that always gets you into trouble?

Tyrell: You always give me a hard time when I talk to Joe in class.

Mr. M.: What is the first thing you need to do to solve this problem of talking in class?

Tyrell: I'm going to solve a problem about talking in class. OK, what is it I have to do?

Mr. M.: What is the next thing to do? What do people do before crossing the street?

Tyrell: I better stop, slow down, and think about what I have to do to solve this problem of talking in class.

Mr. M.: What might you do to keep from talking?

Tyrell: Maybe I'll just keep talking to Joe.

Mr. M.: What might happen if you did that?

Tyrell: Wait, I need to see if that will work. If I keep talking Joe might get mad and tell the teacher. If that happens I will get into trouble. I better think again!

Mr. M.: If you thought your plan was good and it didn't work, what would you do then?

Tyrell: Maybe I should try to not talk and do my work. If I do that I will be able to get my work done.

Mr. M.: What can you do to help you know that your plan will work before you use it?

Tyrell: Is that right? If I stop talking and don't bother Joe, I will get my work done and not get into trouble.

Mr. M.: Will your plan work if you don't use it?

Tyrell: OK, I need to stop talking, sit in my seat, and do my work. First I'll turn my paper and face away from Joe. I won't look at him or talk to him.

Mr. M.: How can you get back on track with your plan after someone has interrupted you and you forgot what you were doing?

Tyrell: I better check to make sure I'm following my plan. OK, I turned my paper and I'm looking away. I'm doing my work and not looking at him. Yes, I'm following my plan.

Mr. M.: Now you have finished your plan. What is the last thing you need to do? What do you say to someone who has done a good job?

Tyrell: Yeah, I'm not talking to my neighbor and I'm doing my work. I had a problem because I was talking to a classmate and not doing my work. But I stopped and thought and came up with a good plan. I did a good job! This really works!

EFFECTIVENESS OF THE COGNITIVE-BEHAVIORAL APPROACH

Evaluations of the effects of CBT with this population have met with mixed results in terms of children's academic achievement, as well as parent and teacher ratings of behavior and social functioning. This has been due, in part, to the time-limited nature of the interventions and the specific structure of research protocols. Such approaches continue to evolve and improve; follow-up research is needed to assess their full impact and long-term effectiveness.

A child with ADD who has learned self-statements to address problems in school often remembers nearly the entire script, even after the trainer and the prompts have been removed. But if the child loses sight of the importance of self-monitoring and self-evaluation, inappropriate behavior can easily resurface. To maintain gains made through CBT, the teacher will need to continue to prompt the child to use the new skills. Prompting can take a number of forms: hand signals, signs posted on the walls, note cards at the child's desk, and/ or laminated cue cards that the student can carry from place to place. To help the skills generalize to a wide variety of settings—the classroom, playground, lunchroom, or bus—the teacher may need to show others who have contact with the child how to use prompts and evaluate the child's use of self-instructions.

In conclusion, CBT ambitiously seeks to modify not only the mind-set of the child with ADD, but also the orientation of the individuals with whom the child has constant contact. Although the training may focus specifically on inappropriate classroom behavior, it is essential that the education process be ongoing and that the skills and the settings in which they are practiced be consistently expanded.

References

Asher, M. J., & Schleser, R. (1988). *Self-instructional manual for teachers and other professionals working with Attention Deficit Hyperactivity Disorder children.* Unpublished manuscript, Illinois Institute of Technology, Chicago.

Braswell, L., & Bloomquist, M. L. (1991). *Cognitive-behavioral therapy with ADHD children: Children, family, and school interventions.* New York: Guilford.

Meichenbaum, D., & Goodman, J. (1971). Training impulsive children to talk to themselves: A means of developing self-control. *Journal of Abnormal Child Psychology, 77,* 115–126.

Schleser, R., Armstrong, K. J., & Allen, J. S. (1990). Attention Deficit Hyperactivity Disorder: New directions. In S. B. Morgan & T. M. Okwumabua (Eds.), *Child and adolescent disorders: Developmental and health psychology perspectives* (pp. 105–133). Hillsdale, NJ: Erlbaum.

Schleser, R., Cohen, R., Meyer, A. W., & Rodick, J. D. (1984). The effects of cognitive level and training procedures on the generalization of self-instructions. *Cognitive Therapy and Research, 8,* 187–200.

Schleser, R., Meyer, A. W., Cohen, R., & Thackwray, D. (1983). Self-instruction interventions with non-self-controlled children: Effects of Discovery versus Faded Rehearsal. *Journal of Consulting and Clinical Psychology, 51,* 954–955.

Vygotsky, L. S. (1962). *Thoughts and language.* New York: MIT Press.

11 Future Directions

Regardless of the extent of a teacher's or mental health professional's experience, there will always be the need to improvise and go beyond the data in the attempt to enhance a child's school success. On the front lines, classroom teachers cannot wait for definitive scientific answers—current problems call for solutions now. Coping with the daily problems and frustrations presented by children with ADD, classroom teachers and parents often have to make decisions based not only on facts but also on intuition. Inasmuch as today's speculations may be tomorrow's science, it is useful to consider a number of trends in ADD assessment, diagnosis, and intervention.

ASSESSMENT AND DIAGNOSIS

Four distinct trends seem to be occurring within the area of assessment and diagnosis. These concern a movement toward identification of ADD in both younger and older groups, the impact of medical technology on the number of children with ADD, reconceptualization of the ADD diagnosis, and development of more objective assessments.

Identification of ADD in Younger and Older Populations

An increasing number of children are being referred for ADD at an earlier age. It is not uncommon for the question of ADD to be raised for some children while they are still in preschool. As noted in chapter 3, it is difficult to make a diagnosis at this young age because so many ADD symptoms are characteristic of the normal preschooler.

Teacher-completed behavior rating scales, naturalistic observations, and objective tests are extremely valuable.

The increase in early identification may be due in part to greater awareness and acceptance of ADD by preschool teachers, pediatricians, and parents. Numerous teacher training programs, reports in the general media, and publications in professional journals have undoubtedly contributed to this increased awareness. Another factor contributing to early identification has been federal legislation mandating preschool programs for children with disabilities. Local school districts, reaching out to identify children with developmental problems, have promoted early identification of ADD and thus ensured the enrollment of more preschool children. In the past, many families may have had the option of keeping their preschool children at home. However, along with the increase in dual-career households has come an increasing demand for child care. As a result, many more preschoolers will come in contact with early childhood professionals capable of screening for a wide variety of problems.

Early identification of ADD is a trend likely to continue into the future. There also appears to be a parallel increase in the identification of adolescents and adults with ADD. This is due in part to greater awareness on the part of teachers, physicians, mental health professionals, and the general public. More adolescents presenting with problems of depression, impulse disorders, and/or substance abuse are likely to be identified as having ADD. These problems may be in response to longstanding ADD that has been neither identified nor treated. There will also be an increased focus on adults with ADD. Evidence for this can be seen in a new thrust by Children With Attention Deficit Disorders (CHADD), a major national support group devoting attention to this significant problem. At CHADD meetings, an increasing number of adults are raising questions as to whether or not an ADD diagnosis is appropriate for them. To date, it seems that many of these adults are the parents of children who also have ADD. The first wave of adults so identified will likely be the parents of children with ADD. The second wave of adults will probably be either self-referred or identified by health professionals.

Impact of Medical Technology

Advancing medical technology has contributed to the survival of many children who, in previous generations, might have failed to do so. Many with a history of premature birth and/or significant complications now enter school with a wide range of disabilities, ADD among them. In response, communities are likely to expand the services of early intervention programs, now conducted within local hospitals and designed for children from birth to age 3. These programs already contribute greatly to the identification and treatment of a wide range of developmental disabilities in very young children.

Although the link between parental substance abuse and ADD is as yet unclear, such programs will also meet the needs of children whose parents abused alcohol, cocaine, heroin, or other drugs. Many clinical histories of children with ADD note that one or both biological parents did in fact have a drug problem, and ADD is likely to be more firmly linked to parental substance abuse as time goes on.

Reconceptualization of the ADD Diagnosis

The third trend relates to a revised view of the descriptive symptoms of ADD. At the time of this writing, the current *Diagnostic and Statistical Manual of Mental Disorders* (DSM-III-R; American Psychiatric Association, 1987) lists Attention Deficit Hyperactivity Disorder (ADHD) as the primary diagnosis and Undifferentiated Attention Deficit Disorder (UADD) as a secondary diagnosis. The previous edition of the *Diagnostic and Statistical Manual* (DSM-III; American Psychiatric Association, 1980) clearly distinguished ADD with hyperactivity (ADD/+H) from ADD without hyperactivity (ADD/−H). The DSM-IV, due for publication in 1994, will once again have a diagnosis that identifies ADD without hyperactivity. Consideration will also be given to discriminating inattention from impulsivity (American Psychiatric Association, 1993; Task Force on DSM-IV, 1991).

It remains unclear which specific symptoms and how many will be required to make a diagnosis within the DSM-IV framework. At some point in the future, it is also possible that other behavioral factors (e.g., aggression) will be considered when making a differential diagnosis. Identification of specific characteristics that allow us to predict responsiveness to treatment and future adjustment will greatly enhance our ability to provide comprehensive treatment.

Development of More Objective Assessments

The fourth trend concerns the development of more reliable, objective measures of ADD. At present, subjective interpretations are relied upon heavily in clinical interviews, naturalistic observations, and even behavior rating scales. In spite of its scientific appearance, a rating scale still relies on a teacher's and/or parent's perceptions.

In addition, the designations of frequency or intensity ("Not at all," "Just a little," "Pretty much," or "Very much") are less than precise. In an attempt to address this problem, a number of more objective approaches have been used, unfortunately with little success. These have included specific subtests from standardized IQ tests as well as tests of cognitive impulsivity (e.g., the Matching Familiar Figures Test; Kagan, 1966a, 1966b). More recently, computerized assessments have been used to screen and diagnose children, adolescents, and even adults with ADD. Of great value because of its ease of administration and empirical support is the Test of Variables of Attention (T.O.V.A.; Greenberg, 1991), discussed in chapter 5. Not only does this method assist in making a definitive diagnosis, it also allows for the determination of a child's responsiveness to medication. Computerized assessments will continue to develop as scientists examine sustained attention to both visual and auditory stimuli.

INTERVENTION

The main trends in intervention for ADD include changes in the way stimulant medication is employed, enhancement of behavioral and cognitive-behavioral approaches to treatment, emphasis on comprehensive education for families, and changes in educational accommodations.

New Approaches to Administering Stimulant Medication

Although a cornerstone of treatment for ADD, the use of stimulant medication continues to meet with resistance due to the misconceptions of teachers, parents, and even clinicians. It is of interest to note that as use of an assessment tool such as the T.O.V.A. becomes more widespread and the effectiveness of stimulant medication becomes easier to document, this resistance may be overcome. This is not to say that behavioral methods will be deemphasized, but rather to suggest that the improved ability to document the effectiveness of medication will likely result in parents' increased willingness to accept a challenge dose for their child.

Another trend is greater use of stimulant medication for children before the age of 6. Although stimulant medication has not generally been recommended for preschool children, clinical experience indicates significant improvement in attention, concentration, and the ability to inhibit impulsive responding for this population. A cautionary note is in order for this group, as well as for children with severe developmental disabilities mistakenly labeled as ADD, whose response to stimulant medication may be poor. Further research is needed to address the specific needs of both these groups.

Increased attention is also being directed toward combining medications. For example, stimulant medication (e.g., methylphenidate) in combination with antidepressant medication (e.g., desipramine) has led to significant gains in some cases where marginal improvement has resulted from use of a single medication. Future research is also needed here to determine which children respond best to which medication or combination of medications.

Finally, the next generation of children with ADD may witness the use of medications that have not yet been used with this population. Various approaches, whether they involve new uses for existing medications or the discovery of new medications, will likely help children function more effectively.

Enhancement of Behavioral and Cognitive-Behavioral Approaches

There has been some disillusionment in recent years regarding the use of cognitive-behavioral approaches (e.g., Social Problem Solving and self-instruction). The overall effectiveness of these approaches in terms of their strength, durability, and generalizability has not been proven as was originally expected (Barkley, 1990). Initial treatment gains have typically not been maintained once the interventions are withdrawn, and when gains are maintained, rarely do they generalize from one behavior or situation to another. There are three possible reasons. First, cognitive-behavior therapists believed that behavioral interventions alone were labor intensive and had little potential for generalization. As a result, cognitive-behavioral interventions replaced more narrow behavioral approaches, and the benefits of these behavioral interventions were lost. Second, cognitive interventions were generally short term, lasting either several weeks or several months, rarely for an extended period of time. Finally, the adults responsible for the children in various environments (e.g., home, school, playground, scouts) were rarely included in the training program.

In order to enhance the effectiveness of cognitive-behavioral approaches, teachers and others must realize that training and prompting must extend over a long period of time. To facilitate change in the child's cognitive repertoire, training should also include parents, teachers, aides, and other significant adults in the child's environment.

Teachers play an integral role in facilitating or inhibiting a child's social and cognitive development through the teacher-child interactive process (Schleser, Armstrong, & Allen, 1990). Given this important role, teachers are best viewed as an ongoing natural resource for cognitive-behavioral interventions. As a result, there is a special need to include teachers in social problem solving and self-instructional training approaches. In a recent study (Asher, 1989), a program was developed to train teachers to use self-instruction with children diagnosed as having ADD. After 21 weeks of training, results indicated that the children's performance in academic tasks and general behavior significantly improved. In post-training evaluations, all the teachers believed that, with the continued use of self-instruction, the remaining problems these children had in other settings and situations could be remediated. Although this study involved only a small number of teachers and no control group, it does suggest that the long-term use of self-instruction and other cognitive-behavioral interventions can have an impact on children's behavior. The greatest promise appears to be the integration of behavioral approaches with cognitive approaches. Future applications will also need to provide for long-term prompting to help these children continue to use the cognitive strategies they have learned.

Emphasis on Educating Families

Another intervention trend will be an increased emphasis on educating families and their children about the nature of ADD. Just as for a child diagnosed with diabetes, a complete reeducation of the family as to the nature of ADD—its causes, development, and treatment—is required. Often when children with ADD are questioned, they refer to stimulant medication as their "good behavior pill," with little understanding of its purpose or, more importantly, what they need to do to help the overall treatment work. Many excellent books and videotapes are already available for families and children. (See the list of selected readings and videotape programs at the back of this book.)

Educational Accommodations

The final trend in intervention concerns educational accommodations. Public Law 94–142 and Section 504 of the Rehabilitation Act now provide for free and appropriate public education for all children with disabilities. When these laws were originally written, the effects of ADD on school-age children were largely misunderstood;

therefore, ADD was not written into the original law. Recently, the Department of Education has clarified the role of the state and local education associations with regard to ADD. We anticipate that legislation will continue to fine-tune the conditions under which the educational needs of children with ADD must be met. Unfortunately, we also would anticipate certain adversarial situations arising between parents and school systems, resulting in litigation and due process to clarify educational needs on a case-by-case basis.

Finally, as more children are identified as having ADD and are mainstreamed into regular classrooms, we will witness increased training and involvement of classroom teachers. We hope that by integrating the material in this book into their daily classroom interactions, all teachers will be in a better position to meet the challenge of the child with ADD.

References

American Psychiatric Association. (1980). *Diagnostic and statistical manual of mental disorders* (3rd ed.). Washington, DC: Author.

American Psychiatric Association. (1987). *Diagnostic and statistical manual of mental disorders* (3rd ed. rev.). Washington, DC: Author.

American Psychiatric Association. (1993). *DSM-IV draft criteria: 3/1/93.* Washington, DC: Author.

Asher, M. J. (1989). *Self-instructional training for teachers and other professionals working with Attention Deficit Disorder children.* Unpublished doctoral dissertation, Illinois Institute of Technology, Chicago.

Barkley, R. A. (1990). *Attention Deficit Hyperactivity Disorder: A handbook for diagnosis and treatment.* New York: Guilford.

Greenberg, L. M. (1991). *T.O.V.A. interpretation manual: Test of Variables of Attention computer program.* Minneapolis: University of Minnesota.

Kagan, J. (1966a). Modifiability of an impulsive tempo. *Journal of Educational Psychology, 57,* 359–365.

Kagan, J. (1966b). Reflection-impulsivity: The generality and dynamics of conceptual tempo. *Journal of Abnormal Psychology, 71,* 17–24.

Schleser, R., Armstrong, K. J., & Allen, J. S. (1990). Attention Deficit Hyperactivity Disorder: New directions. In S. B. Morgan & T. M. Okwumabua (Eds.), *Child and adolescent disorders: Developmental and health psychology perspectives* (pp. 105–133). Hillsdale, NJ: Erlbaum.

Task Force on DSM-IV. (1991). *DSM-IV options book: Work in progress: 9/1/91.* Washington, DC: American Psychiatric Press.

Assessment and Recording Forms

Student Observation Scorecard for Frequency

Student _____ Observer _____

Target behavior _____

Week of _____ Time of observation _____

Day	Target behavior (number of times)
Monday	_____
Tuesday	_____
Wednesday	_____
Thursday	_____
Friday	_____
Total times this week	_____
Average per day	_____

Student Observation Scorecard for Duration

Student _____ Observer _____

Target behavior _____

Week of _____ Time of observation _____

Day	Target behavior (number of minutes)
Monday	_____
Tuesday	_____
Wednesday	_____
Thursday	_____
Friday	_____
Total minutes this week	_____
Average per day	_____

Student Observation Scorecard for Time Sampling

Student _____ Observer _____

Target behavior _____

Week of _____ Time of observation _____

Period of time sampled _____

Day	Target behavior (+/−)	Daily percentage
Monday		_____ %
Tuesday		_____ %
Wednesday		_____ %
Thursday		_____ %
Friday		_____ %

Weekly average _____ %

ABC Analysis Form

Student _____ Observer _____ Date _____

Antecedents	Behavior	Consequences
1.	1.	1.
2.	2.	2.
3.	3.	3.
4.	4.	4.
5.	5.	5.
6.	6.	6.

Reinforcement Inventory

Name _____ Age/grade _____

Completed by _____ Date _____

1. Who is your favorite adult at school?

   _____

2. What is your favorite school subject?

   _____

3. What are three things you most enjoy in school?

   _____

   _____

   _____

4. What school activity would you most enjoy doing
   with a friend?

   _____

5. While in school, what would you like to do if you had a
   chance?

   _____

6. What school activity would you most enjoy doing with your
   teacher?

   _____

7. What is the best reward a teacher can give you?

   _____

8. What weekend activity do you most enjoy?

   _____

9. If your teacher gave you free time to do anything you wanted
   to do in the classroom, what would you do?

   _____

10. Below is a list of privileges or activities that some students
    enjoy. Please circle the items you would like.

Note: Teachers may compile their own list of privileges or activities to include reinforcers
appropriate to the student's developmental level (see Tables 8.1 and 8.2 for examples).

SELP Daily Scorecard

Name _____ Date _____

Please rate this student on his or her performance in your classroom in each category listed. Use the following scale:

    4 = Excellent
    2 = Fair
    0 = Poor
    X = Not applicable

Category					Class period						
	1	2	3	4	5	6	7	8	9	10	Total
Follows class rules											
Completes class-work or participates in class											
Completes homework											
Gets along with other students											
Teacher's initials											
Total											

Comments

SELP Reward Menu for Home/School Privileges

Name _____ Date _____

Basic privileges	Points required
1.	
2.	
3.	
4.	

Special privileges	Points required
1.	
2.	
3.	
4.	
5.	
6.	
7.	
8.	
9.	
10.	
11.	
12.	

SELP Weekly Record Sheet

Name _____

Week beginning _____

Points required for basic privileges _____

Points carried over from previous week _____

Day	Points earned	Points spent	Savings
Monday	_____	_____	_____
Tuesday	_____	_____	_____
Wednesday	_____	_____	_____
Thursday	_____	_____	_____
Friday	_____	_____	_____
Saturday	Basic privileges free	_____	_____
Sunday	Basic privileges free	_____	_____

Selected Readings and Videotape Programs

General Background

Barkley, R. A. (1990). *Attention Deficit Hyperactivity Disorder: A handbook for diagnosis and treatment.* New York: Guilford.
Copeland, E. (1991). *Medications for attention disorders and related medical problems.* Atlanta: 3C's of Childhood.

Assessment

Barkley, R. A. (1991). *Attention Deficit Hyperactivity Disorder: A clinical workbook.* New York: Guilford.
Conners, C. K. (1989). *Conners' Teacher Rating Scales manual.* North Tonawanda, NY: Multi-Health Systems.
Goyette, C. H., Conners, C. K., & Ulrich, R. F. (1978). Normative data on revised Conners' Parent and Teacher Rating Scales. *Journal of Abnormal Child Psychology, 6,* 221–236.
Greenberg, L. M. (1991). *T.O.V.A. interpretation manual: Test of Variables of Attention computer program.* Minneapolis: University of Minnesota.
Keefe, F. J., Kopel, S. A., & Gordon, S. B. (1978). *A practical guide to behavioral assessment.* New York: Springer.

For Teachers

Asher, M., & Schleser, R. (1988). *Self-instructional manual for teachers and other professionals working with Attention Deficit Hyperactivity Disorder children.* Unpublished manuscript, Illinois Institute of Technology, Chicago.

Bandura, A. (1977). *Social learning theory.* Englewood Cliffs, NJ: Prentice-Hall.

Braswell, L., & Bloomquist, M. L. (1991). *Cognitive-behavior therapy with ADHD children: Child, family and school interventions.* New York: Guilford.

Children With Attention Deficit Disorders. (1988). *Attention deficit disorders: A guide for teachers.* Plantation, FL: Author.

Copeland, E. D., & Love, V. (1990). *Attention without tension: A teacher's handbook on attention disorders (ADHD and ADD).* Atlanta: 3C's of Childhood.

Ginsburg, H., & Opper, S. (1969). *Piaget's theory of intellectual development.* Englewood Cliffs, NJ: Prentice Hall.

Meichenbaum, D. H., & Asarnow, J. (1979). Cognitive-behavior modification and metacognitive development: Implications for the classroom. In P. C. Kendall & S. Hollon (Eds.), *Cognitive-behavioral interventions: Theory, research and procedures.* New York: Academic.

Meyers, A., & Craighead, W. E. (1984). *Cognitive-behavior therapy with children.* New York: Plenum.

Paine, S. C., Radicchi, J., Rosellini, L. C., Deutchman, L., & Darch, C. B. (1983). *Structuring your classroom for academic success.* Champaign, IL: Research Press.

Schleser, R., Armstrong, K. J., & Allen, J. S. (1990). Attention Deficit Hyperactivity Disorder: New directions. In S. B. Morgan & T. M. Okwumabua (Eds.), *Child and adolescent disorders: Developmental and health psychology perspectives* (pp. 105–133). Hillsdale, NJ: Erlbaum.

Vygotsky, L. S. (1962). *Thoughts and language.* New York: MIT Press.

Zentall, S. (1992). *Identification, assessment and management of ADHD youth in educational contexts.* Paper presented at the fourth annual conference on Attention Deficit Disorder (CHADD), Chicago.

For Parents

Fowler, M. (1990). *Maybe you know my kid: A parent's guide to identifying, understanding and helping your child with ADHD.* New York: Birchland.

Goldstein, S., & Goldstein, M. (1989). *Why won't my child pay attention?* Salt Lake City, UT: Neurology, Learning and Behavior Center.

Gordon, M. (1990). *ADHD/hyperactivity: A consumer's guide.* New York: GSI.

Greenberg, G. S., & Horn, W. F. (1991). *Attention Deficit Hyperactivity Disorder: Questions and answers for parents.* Champaign, IL: Research Press.

Parker, H. (1989). *The ADD hyperactivity workbook for parents, teachers and kids.* Plantation, FL: Impact.

Silver, L. (1984). *The misunderstood child: A guide for parents of LD children.* New York: McGraw-Hill.

For Children

Galvin, M. (1988). *Otto learns about his medicine.* New York: Magination.
Gordon, M. (1991). *Jumpin' Johnny get back to work: A child's guide to ADHD/ hyperactivity.* DeWitt, NY: GSI.
Moss, D. (1989). *Shelly, the hyperactive turtle.* Kensington, MD: Woodbine.
Parker, R., & Parker, H. (1992). *Making the grade: An adolescent's struggle with Attention Deficit Disorder.* Plantation, FL: Impact.
Quinn, P. O., & Stern, J. (1991). *Putting on the brakes.* New York: Magination.

Videotape Programs

Barkley, R. A. (1992). *ADHD: What do we know?* New York: Guilford.
Barkley, R. A. (1992). *ADHD: What can we do?* New York: Guilford.
Copeland, E. D. (1989). *Understanding attention disorders: Preschool through adult.* Atlanta: 3C's of Childhood.
Goldstein, S., & Goldstein, M. (1991). *It's just attention disorder: A video guide for kids.* Salt Lake City: Neurology, Learning and Behavior Center.
Phelan, T. (1990). *Attention Deficit Hyperactivity Disorder.* Glen Ellyn, IL: Child Management Press.

Index

About the Authors

Dr. Steven B. Gordon received his Ph.D. in clinical psychology from West Virginia University and was a postdoctoral fellow in behavior modification at the State University of New York at Stony Brook. He has served as clinical associate professor in the Department of Psychiatry, Robert Wood Johnson Medical School, and is a Diplomate in Behavior Therapy and in Behavioral Psychology, American Board of Professional Psychology. Currently, Dr. Gordon is a licensed psychologist in private practice and Director of Behavior Therapy Associates, P.A., in Somerset, New Jersey. He is also a contributing faculty member at the Graduate School of Applied and Professional Psychology, Rutgers University, where he teaches behavior therapy. Dr. Gordon has consulted with numerous school districts and private special education schools. He also lectures extensively and conducts workshops for parents and teachers on the topic of Attention Deficit Disorder.

Dr. Michael J. Asher received his Ph.D. in clinical psychology from the Illinois Institute of Technology in Chicago. A licensed psychologist in private practice at Behavior Therapy Associates, P.A., in Somerset, New Jersey, Dr. Asher is also a consultant to numerous school districts and private schools in New Jersey and a field supervisor for the Graduate School of Applied and Professional Psychology at Rutgers University. In addition, he conducts workshops at the local, state, and national levels on the topic of Attention Deficit Disorder and other disorders in children and adolescents.